Languages and Language
in Black Africa

Pierre Alexandre

Translated by
F. A. LEARY

Northwestern University Press

Evanston   1972

Originally published in French under the title
Langues et langage en Afrique noire,
copyright © 1967 by Payot, Paris.

Pierre Alexandre is a Professor at L'Ecole des Langues
Orientales at the University of Paris.

F. A. Leary is Assistant Professor of History at Temple
University.

Contents

Preface to the American Edition   v
Author's Preface   vii

CHAPTER I: QUIS, QUID, QUO, QUANDO, QUOMODO, QUANTUM?   1

CHAPTER II: AFRICAN LINGUISTICS: WHY, WHAT FOR, HOW?   19

CHAPTER III: SURELY NO ONE SPEAKS AN AFRICAN LANGUAGE, DO
    THEY?   31
1. Class Languages: Bantu   39
2. Non-Bantu Languages without Classes: West Atlantic Group   46
3. Languages without Classes: Hamito-Semitic Family (?)   48
4. Languages without Classes: Nilo-Saharan Family   53
5. Languages without Classes: Mande Group   54
6. Languages without Classes: Kwa Group   56
7. Trade Languages: Pidgins and Creoles   59

CHAPTER IV: FROM TRIBES TO NATIONS: PROBLEMS OF COMMUNI-
    CATION   73

CHAPTER V: THE SPOKEN WORD AND THE WRITTEN WORD   103

CHAPTER VI: SINCE WE MUST CONCLUDE: JOIN LINGUISTICS AND
    SEE THE WORLD!   123

Selected Bibliography   125
Appendix: Special Characters Most Frequently Used in the
    Transcription of African Languages   129

Index   131

MAP 1. Official and National Languages of Africa   15

MAP 2. Sketch of Language Families in Africa   71

Preface to the American Edition

The American edition of this book differs slightly from the French original. Following the British reviewers' advice, some highly technical passages were removed from Chapter III. They could—as the London zoo keeper told the nice old lady—be of interest only to another rhinoceros.

Other changes had to be made with a view to what can be called cultural, rather than linguistic, adaptation. It was in most cases rather easy to find English equivalents for phonetic or even structural French examples. In other domains, "translation" was far more difficult, as, for instance, when it came to finding an American counterpart for France's Elder Crooner, M. Tino Rossi. This led to some arduous exercises in applied anthropology; and, while both F. A. Leary and myself had done field work in West Africa, we had but a tourist's knowledge of each other's countries. One of the results was a continuous flow of letters between us—and, later on, Mrs. Seidman, of Northwestern University Press—to settle such fine points as whether "Canuck" could be considered a sociological and psychological equivalent of "Boche" or—*caveant censores*—whether *sikuru* could be substituted for *tiraku*. I must confess that Miss Leary (by the way, she is *not* responsible for the brand of English used in this prefatory note) showed considerable pluck and grit in battling with my rather idiosyncratic French. I cannot thank her enough for her work. Thanks are due, too, to Professors Jack Berry, of Northwestern University, and Malcolm Guthrie, of the School of Oriental and African Studies, University of London, who very kindly undertook a revision of the more technical aspects of this book. May I add that the latter was also my introducer to Bantu linguistics and that I owe him more than I can ever thank him for?

PIERRE ALEXANDRE

August, 1971

Author's Preface

Does one need excuses for writing a book, and especially a book on African languages? Possibly so. At any rate here are some:

There was that time when my phone rang and a woman's voice said, "This is the X hospital calling. Are you the professor of African?" "African?" "Well, of the African language, you know. We have an African here in the emergency ward, and he speaks no French. The intern called the university, and they told us that at the School of Oriental Languages. . . ."

And then there was that old school friend, whom I hadn't seen since graduation till I met him in the Classics Department twenty years later: "What is it, exactly, that you're teaching? Bantu languages? You've really got it made. Boy, that's a soft job!"

And also that official of exalted rank: "African languages? Come now, professor, those languages are dying out. They all speak French like you and me."

Only three anecdotes from among hundreds that all tell the same story. I have written this book partially in the hope of stopping the repetition of such nonsense.

This is not a study of African languages, for such an endeavor would interest hardly anyone except Africanist linguists; it would probably not interest even general linguists. This book concerns the languages of Africa and the cultural, political, or economic problems which they raise, as well as the wider scientific and human problems. The term "Africa" is used here in the parochial and personal sense where the uninitiated would say "Tropical Africa" or, worse, "Africa south of the Sahara."

I do not pretend that I shall resolve all the problems raised by African languages or even generally suggest solutions to them. In most cases, this is a right and a responsibility which belong only to the Africans themselves. After all, considering my position, I can do no more than give a brief survey of the main lines of these problems or simply point out that a problem exists. Even this is a large task in a subject widely ignored by the educated public and by the Africans themselves.

I have tried as much as possible to avoid the technical jargon of the linguist or the anthropologist. Wherever I have had to use such terms,

I have given a brief definition, as clear as possible and illustrated by concrete examples. I have certainly not succeeded in making everything crystal clear to the uninitiated, just as I have probably not satisfied the specialists. It is difficult to simplify without becoming senseless. I have preferred to put my confidence in the reader and to ask him to make the slight effort necessary for understanding the various problems. I would have insulted the reader and prostituted myself by offering the Africa of Tarzan or Little Black Sambo.

PIERRE ALEXANDRE

Paris–Abidjan–Ibadan
1963–1964

Languages and Language
in Black Africa

CHAPTER I

Quis, Quid, Quo, Quando, Quomodo, Quantum?

Numerical uncertainties: 200 languages or 1,200? Reasons or excuses for these uncertainties. The "major" languages: forces favoring their diffusion. A tentative summary of the main languages. Problems of linguistic geography and stratigraphy.

The first problem in dealing with the languages of Africa concerns their number: How many languages are there? For this reason, this book opens with an admission of ignorance: I can give no answer to this question, and no respectable linguist would be any more willing to offer a precise number.

One can, nevertheless, make estimates, varying from 200 or 250 to more than 1,200. Many factors cause this uncertainty. First, there are theoretical factors: specialists have not yet agreed on the general criteria distinguishing a language from a dialect or on the application of these criteria to the different languages found in the field. They tend to increase or diminish the length of their list according to their own opinion on the question. Where Delafosse, for example, saw one language (Mande or Mandingo), which he divided into dialects, Westermann saw a group of ten languages. Then there are also practical reasons: until several years ago most studies of African languages were the work of amateurs, a small group and one often lacking appropriate training. The information they gathered was occasionally vague. A language from whose vocabulary we know only a few words may be found on a list under two or three different names, while another name on the same list may actually refer to several different languages. Certain languages noted by one explorer always appear on the lists, although we may know only their names, which may themselves have been incorrectly registered.

We should remember, and thus acquit both past and present linguists, that a linguistic census is often a difficult endeavor. The name that one people calls itself may differ from the name given their language: for example, the Ashanti of Ghana speak Twi. The Kotokoli of Togo speak Tem. The Fulbe (whom we call Fulani) speak Fulfulde, etc. The problem becomes more complicated when the information is gathered at second hand, for frequently a tribe designates its neighbor or its neighbor's language by terms which are not only incorrect but also offensive. Imagine, for instance, an African explorer interrogating New England Yankees about their northern neighbors. He would conclude that the northern side of the Canadian border was peopled with [frɔgiz] and [kanɔks] speaking [frog] or [frenci]. Then, if later he should also meet a real Quebecois speaking [frãsɛ], his classification of languages for this part of America would be singularly incorrect. However, I know of strictly analogous examples in classifications of African languages.

My own estimate, which is no more valid than any other, places the approximate number of African languages at around 800. My basis for this conclusion comes primarily, but not uniquely, from a critical examination of the recent classifications made by Westermann, Bryan, Guthrie, and Greenberg. Knowing the methodologies of these linguists and taking as samples of their classifications the regions where I have worked myself, I arrive at a distinctly smaller total than the 1,200 which would result from adding Guthrie's classification (of Bantu languages) to Greenberg's (of African languages excluding Bantu).

Eight hundred languages nevertheless represents an enormous figure for a continent where the population probably does not exceed 200 million inhabitants. Furthermore, the part which I am discussing does not include the Mediterranean region, containing about 40 million people with great linguistic homogeneity (Arabic; Berber), nor the Ethiopian mountains and the Somalian horn, where there are about 20 million additional people speaking languages classified by Greenberg as "Afro-Asiatic" ("Hamito-Semitic," in European studies; related to Arabic and Berber). This leaves "my" Africa with some 150 million inhabitants and about 750 languages.

One overly simplistic division would indicate that each language probably includes 200,000 speakers. This evidently means nothing, for one finds that in reality these languages cover a wide gamut, extending on the one side from languages found in only a few villages and among several dozen speakers (these are often among the most interesting on the level of theoretical linguistics) to those understood by several million people spread throughout an area comparable to that of western Europe. At one end is Kaaloŋ, still spoken by two hundred elderly people in a remote Cameroonian district; at the other is Swahili, used for intertribal relations from the Comoro Islands, Zanzibar, Tanganyika,[1] Kenya, part of Uganda, along both banks of the Congo, and even in Somalia and Zambia. Historical and sociological factors are the principal reasons behind language extension and diffusion, in Africa as elsewhere. These historical and sociological factors, in Africa perhaps more than elsewhere, depend in turn on geographical conditions.

Languages with the widest spread are found especially in the savanna zones or in partially wooded plateaus, where communications and life are relatively easy and where, prior to the colonial era, important traditional states developed. The existence and development of these states generally resulted from the creation and maintenance of active commercial routes.

Equally noticeable, on the other hand, is the great linguistic fragmentation found in mountainous and forest regions. Most frequently these were regions where communication was difficult and population was sparse and where, in addition, there were many refugee groups who fled from a victorious enemy and who, because of the communications difficulties, were subsequently prevented from reconstituting social groups on any large scale.

In reality, the most widespread languages generally demonstrate such a great diversity of dialects that—as I mentioned above, with Delafosse's opinion on Mande—one hesitates to consider them as constituting single entities. An important unifying factor lies in the existence of a transcription covering the total or the greatest part of their field of extension. Orthographic unity, especially where the language thus transcribed is used in schools, facilitates the creation of a group of received forms, understood, although not always used, by the majority of speakers of the different dialects. The most typical case of this is Swahili, whose standard form is regulated by an international committee with headquarters presently at Makerere University in Uganda.[2] The authority of this committee is recognized in all the former British colonies of East Africa and to a limited extent in the Congo-Leo (Kinshasa). Yoruba and Hausa also benefit from this kind of standardization, but only in Nigeria, since the schools in neighboring countries (Dahomey and Niger Republic) use only French.

1. Zanzibar and Tanganyika merged to form Tanzania in 1964.
2. Transferred since 1964 to University College, Dar es Salaam (Tanzania).

Different and rival religious missions representing different faiths have often adopted nonunified transcriptions for closely related languages or dialects and have thus worked in the opposite direction. This has contributed to consolidating linguistic heterogeneity, which is further aggravated in certain cases by religious opposition symbolized by orthographic differences. Where rivalries between missions have been particularly intense, one language may have been influenced by three, four, or *n* spellings, to which the members of each persuasion attach as great an importance as to their doctrines and dogmas. I prefer to give no examples!

Other nonlinguistic elements play a role in the degree of diffusion of some languages. Such diffusion can (as in the cases of Swahili and Hausa) go beyond the boundaries of the ethnic groups where the languages are indigenous. We shall return to this point in detail later, but the following illustrate the point:

—political or administrative factors: the choice of one language as a national language, official language, or language of instruction.

—the religious factor: adoption of one language for evangelization.

—the economic factor: diffusion of a language by an ethnic group specializing in trade (or a special activity) (Hausa, Mande-Dyula).

—sociological factors, often combining the above: "prestige" languages, such as Fulfulde (Fulani) in Northern Cameroon; languages showing social difference or social distance: the use of Songhaï-Jerma in Kumasi by migrants with different origins.

At the present time (early 1964) only three states have actually adopted an African language as a national language: Zanzibar and Tanganyika (Swahili), and Northern Nigeria (Hausa). In Togo the adoption of Ewe has remained at the theoretical level. Mauritania has adopted Arabic, the religious language of the vast majority of the population; but this represents a special case to the extent that Mauritania does not form part of Black Africa but tends rather to serve as a transition between Black Africa and North Africa.[3]

There is no correct and complete census of African languages. Such a census, in my opinion, would have little interest except as a strictly technical study. It might, however, be useful to give a list of 52 languages (or very homogeneous dialect or linguistic groups) which comprise or exceed a million speakers. On the regional level this criterion is absurd, for it means excluding many important languages in a

3. In 1966 three other nations adopted African languages: Rwanda (Kinyarwanda), Burundi (Kirundi), and the Central African Republic (Sango). Since that date Lesotho and Botswana have followed suit.

single country because they do not reach that fateful number: for example, in Chad, the different languages called Sara; or, in the Central African Republic, Gbaya, Banda, and Ngbandi—groups which among themselves probably have 750,000 speakers, who extend over the border into Cameroon and Congo-Kinshasa.

At the all-African level (limited to my above definition), I have not mentioned certain important languages: French, English, Arabic, Portuguese, or the Afro-European pidgins of the west coast. The special problems posed by these languages will be discussed below.

Table 1 has been divided along certain lines:

(a) The first name given for a language or a group, or for each language of a group, is the one most often found in technical literature. Following, and in parentheses, are the "popular" or "journalistic" names; then, in italics, comes the transcription of the vernacular names of the language. In showing the principal "popular" names I have generally not resorted to any kinds of decorative varieties introduced to provide exotic spice or pseudoscientific weight, as, for instance, "Peuhl," "Peulh," etc.

(b) The geographical regions are defined broadly by the rather vague terminology currently used:

WA: West African, divided into the Sudanic and forest (or Guinean) zones (in brief, the coastal zone, which is partially forested)

AE: Equatorial African, divided into *western* (Atlantic side), marked W, and *central* (the Congo Basin and the Great Lakes), marked C

CA: Central African, from the Chad Basin to the Nile

EA: East African

SA: South Africa

Next are given the countries where the language is currently spoken.

(c) The number of speakers is estimated roughly in millions or decimal fractions of a million. Indeed, although we sometimes have a rather precise idea of the number of persons speaking a given language as their mother tongue, we are more often obliged to guess, more or less scientifically, at the total number of those who use it as a second or auxiliary language.

(d) The reference to "classification" indicates the position the language occupies in the classifications of Delafosse (French), Westermann (German and English), and Greenberg (American), symbolized (you will have guessed it) by D, W, and G. The sign "T," which appears once or twice, is a reference to Professor A. N. Tucker of London, who is currently engaged in revising and completing Westermann's study.

(e) The available material for each language is coded between 0 and 6:

0: nothing (such is not the case for the major languages)

1: poor: antiquated, incomplete, or very poor grammars or dictionaries; unscientific transcription systems

2: mediocre: more complete works, but outdated on the scientific or technical level; infrequently and poorly commented texts; no mention of tones

3: average: works dating generally from after 1914; approximately accurate phonetic transcriptions; reference to tones; readable, translatable texts

4: quite good: better than average (3)

5: good: works conforming to modern standards; correctly noted tones; phonological and phonetic description; annotated texts

6: better than good (5): abundant materials, stylistic and dialectic studies, audio materials:

D = usable dictionary
G = grammar
T = texts
S = sound (audio) materials (records or tapes)

(f) Uses: this refers to uses other than simple verbal communication of information between persons knowing the language where these have a certain significance or a certain official character:

A = systematic usage for administrative purposes
E = recognized usage in official school system (tolerated usage is not mentioned)
P = usage in the press
R = regular usage on the radio
L = existence of a certain tradition of written literature, other than translations, textbooks, hymnbooks, and catechisms

(g) Observations: complementary remarks considered useful by the author.

I have omitted the "minor" languages—"minor" in terms of the number of their speakers but with enormous interest at the scientific level (except for those languages which enjoy a relative importance on the regional scale although without sufficient speakers to be included among the important languages on the African level). Indeed, some entire groups are not represented on this list. These are for the most part the languages of Central Africa between Lake Chad and the Nile, spoken by small groups of peoples of which very little is known. Africanist linguists may take great pleasure in discussing the classification of Kadugli-Krongo or may win lasting enemies as a result of

TABLE 1

No.	Language or Group*	Geographical Zone	No. of Speakers	Classification	Documentation	Usage	Comments
1.	Akan:* Twi-Fante, Anyi-Baule (Agni-Baoulé)	Guinean WA: Ghana, Ivory Coast	3 M +	D: Eburno-Dahomean W: Kwa D: Kwa	(Twi-Fante) 3 D G T S; Anyi-Baule 1	A E P R (Ghana)	Proposed as the national language for Ghana. Lingua franca in Ivory Coast.
2.	Bini-Edo* (Benin), èdó	Guinean WA: Nigeria (Midwest)	0.8 M +	D: Nigero-Cameroonian W: Kwa G: Kwa	3 — D G T	A E R	Political importance in the Midwest Region of the Federation.
3, 4.	Chokwe—Lunda,* Cokwe, ciLunda	AE (W,C): Congo-K., Angola, Zambia	1 M	D, W: Bantu G: Benue-Congo	3 — D G	E	Chokwe seems to be spreading by absorption of unwritten neighboring languages.
5.	Efik—Ibibio (Calabar)	Guinean WA: E. Nigeria (Niger Delta)	1 M	D: Nigero-Cameroonian W: "Isolated non-class" G: Benue-Congo	4 — D G S	A E R	Traditionally the commercial language of the Lower Niger; presently supplanted by Igbo.
6.	Ewe (Ehoué), Evegbe	Guinean WA: Dahomey, Togo, Ghana	1.5 M	D: Eburno-Dahomean W: Kwa G: Kwa	4 — D G T	A E P R	Theoretically official in Togo. Aŋlɔ and Gɛ lingua francas in Ghana and Togo; Fɔ dialect in Dahomey.
7,	"Pahouin"*	AE (W): Cameroon,	1.5 M +	D, W: Bantu	2 — D G T	P R	The various languages

* Indicates a group.

TABLE 1—*continued*

No.	Language or Group*	Geographical Zone	No. of Speakers	Classification	Docu- mentation	Usage	Comments
8, 9.	Ewondo (Yaounde) —Bulu— Fan (Fang, Pahouin)	Gabon, Rio Muni		G: Benue-Congo			of this group tend to melt into one language, dominant in Gabon, Rio Muni, and in the S. and S.E. Cameroon. Expanding.
10.	Ganda (*luGanda*)	Uganda	2 M	D, W: Bantu G: Benue-Congo	5—D G T S	A E P R L	Progress checked for political reasons.
11.	Hausa (Haoussa)	Sudanic WA: Nigeria, Niger, and isolated groups in all towns of Sudanic West Africa	10 M	D: Nigero-Chadic W: Chado-Hamitic G: Afro-Asiatic E.	6—D G T S	A E P R L	Official language of Northern Nigeria; main lingua franca and commercial language of West Africa; Arabic and Latin transcriptions; significant literature.
12.	Igbo (Ibo)	Guinean WA: E. Nigeria	3.5 M	D: Nigero-Cameroonian W, G: Kwa	5—D G T S	A E P R	Semiofficial language of Eastern Nigeria; expanding.
13.	Kanuri (Kanouri, Bornuan)	CA: N. Nigeria, Niger, Chad (around L. Chad)	2 M	D: Nilo-Chadic W: Hinterland Sudan (T: E. Saharan) G: Nilo-Saharan (lower)	2— G T	A (until 1960)	A language suffering a setback since the decline of the Bornu Empire; Latin and Arabic transcriptions; fairly ancient literature.

#	Language	Region	Population	Classification		A E P R	Notes
14.	Kikuyu (*iGikuyu*)	EA: Kenya	1.8 M + 0.5 M (Embu, Meru)	D, W: Bantu G: Benue-Congo	4 — D G T	A E P R	Demographically and sociologically growing language.
15, 16.	Kisi—Temne*	Guinean WA: Guinea, Liberia, Sierra Leone	Kisi: 0.25 M Bulom-Sherbro: 0.20 M Temne: 0.5 M	D: Senegalo-Guinean W: West Atlantic G: West Atlantic	1 (G) — 2 — 2 (D G)	A E R (Sierra Leone)	
17.	Kongo (Congo), *kiKongo*	AE (W, C): Congo-K., Congo-Brazzaville, Angola	2 M +	D, W: Bantu G: Benue-Congo	5 — D G T	A E P R	Groups divided into many dialects but with common lingua franca forms which function even outside its boundaries.
18.	Kru* (Kroo): Bete, Grebo, Basa	Guinean WA: Liberia, Ivory Coast	0.25 M ?	D: Eburno-Liberian W: Kru G: Kwa	1 — G	R ? (Grebo?)	Very little-known group. A form of Anglicized Grebo seems to serve as the professional language for sailors and fishermen ("Kroo-boys").
19.	Lingala (Bangala)	AE (C): Congo-K., Congo-Brazzaville, Central African Republic	1.5 M	D, W: Bantu G: Benue-Congo	3 — D G S	A E P R	A lingua franca derived from several languages in the Congo Valley. Expanding, to the detriment of Sango.

*Indicates a group.

TABLE 1—*continued*

No.	Language or Group*	Geographical Zone	No. of Speakers	Classification	Documentation	Usage	Comments
20.	Luba (Baluba), *ciLuba*	AE (C): Congo-K. (Kasai, Katanga), Zambia	1.5 M	D, W: Bantu G: Benue-Congo	4 — D G T	A E P R	One of the official languages of the former Belgian Congo.
21.	Luhya, *luLuhya*	EA: Uganda, Kenya	0.8 M	D, W: Bantu G: Benue-Congo	2 — D G	? E (Missions)	
22.	Lwo* (Luo): Luo, Shilluk, Acholi, Alur	CA: Southern Sudan, Ethiopia, Uganda, Congo-K., Kenya, Tanganyika	2 M +, of which 1 M for Luo	D: Nilo-Abyssinian W: Nilotic G: Nilo-Saharan, E 1	2 — D G	A E R (Kenya, Uganda)	In fact, two groups: Lwo of the north and Lwo of the south, the latter being more homogeneous and important. Linguistic conflict: Lwo *vs.* Bantu in Kenya.
23.	Mande-Fu*: Susu — Mende — Kpelle (Guerze) — Loma, etc.	Guinean WA: Guinea, Liberia, Sierra Leone, Ivory Coast	2 M Mende, 0.5	D: Nigero-Senegalese W, G: Mande	1 or 2, D G for some languages	A E (Sierra Leone) R	Peripheral languages, often in the forest or mountainous zones. Much more differentiated than Mande-Tan.
24.	Subgroup: Mande-Tan (Mandingo, Mandinka): Malinke — Bambara — Dyula, Khasonke, etc.	WA: Western Sudan — Senegal, Mali, Gambia, Ivory Coast, Guinea, Upper Volta, Ghana, Sierra Leone (ancient Mali Empire), Liberia	6 M +	D: Nigero-Senegalese W, G: Mande	3 — D G	R	Very important lingua franca, proposed as the official language of Mali. Some texts in Arabic script; *Vai* in Sierra Leone has a special script.
25.	Mossi (Moshi), *Mòrè*	Sudanic WA: Upper Volta, N. Togo, N.E. Ghana	2 M	D: Voltaic W: Gur G: Gur or Voltaic	1 — D G	R	Dominant language in Upper Volta.

No.	Language	Distribution	Speakers	Classification		Notes
26, 27, 28.	Nguni*: Zulu, Xhosa, Swazi *isi Zulu, isi Xhosa, isi Swati*	SA: Republic of South Africa, Rhodesia, Zambia, Mozambique	2 M + 2.5 M + 0.25 M	D, W: Bantu G: Benue-Congo	6—DGTS	Neighboring languages, phonetically influenced by Bushman-Hottentot. Sizable modern literature. Creolized or pidginized dialect: *Kitchen Kaffir (Isipiki or Fanekalo)*.
29.	Nupe	Sudanic WA: N. Nigeria	0.5 M	D: Nigero-Cameroonian W, G: Kwa	2—DGT AE (until 1960) R	Some texts transcribed with Arabic scripts.
30, 31.	Nyanja—Cewa, *ciNyanja, ciCewa*	EA: Malawi, Mozambique, Rhodesia, Zambia	1 M	D, W: Bantu G: Benue-Congo	2—DG AEPR	Nyanja is the main language of Malawi.
32.	Fula (Ful, Peul, Fulani, Toucouleur, Poular, etc.), *Fulfulde*	WA (C): Western and central Sudan from Senegal to the Nile: esp. Senegal, Guinea, Mali, Upper Volta, Niger, Nigeria, Cameroon	5 M +	D: Senegalo-Guinean W, G: West Atlantic	4—DGT A (Nigeria) PRL	Lingua franca and prestige language in N. Cameroon; Arabic and Latin transcriptions. Sizable literature.
33, 34.	Ronga—Tsonga (Thonga), *siRonga, siTsonga*	SA: Mozambique, Rhodesia, Republic of South Africa	1.25 M	D, W: Bantu G: Benue-Congo	2—DG ? E	
35, 36.	Rwanda—Rundi, *Runyarwanda, ikiRundi*	EA: Rwanda, Burundi, Congo-K., Uganda, Tanganyika	5 M	D, W: Bantu G: Benue-Congo	3—DGT AEPRL	Rwanda and Rundi are in fact two dialects of a single language. Part of the oral literature has been transcribed.

*Indicates a group.

TABLE 1—continued

No.	Language or Group*	Geographical Zone	No. of Speakers	Classification	Docu- mentation	Usage	Comments
37.	Sango (Songo, Sangho)	CA: Central African Republic, South Chad	1.5 M	D: Ubangian W: Nigritic	1 — G	A R	Lingua franca derived from *Ngbandi*. National language of the Central African Republic (1965).
38.	Senufo (Senoufo)	Sudanic WA: Upper Ivory Coast, N. Ghana, Upper Volta, Mali	1 M	D: Voltaic W: Gur	1 — G	R	
39.	Shona (Chishona)	EA: Mozambique, Rhodesia	1 M	D, W: Bantu G: Benue-Congo	4 — D G T	A E P R L	Shona is the result of concerted efforts at unifying various re-lated languages and dialects since 1929.
40.	Songhaï (Sonray, Songhoï), *Sonray*, Dialect Jerma, Dendi	WA: Western Sudan, Niger Valley: Mali, Upper Volta, Niger, N. Dahomey, N. Nigeria	1 M +	D: Nigero-Senegalese W: Songhay G: Nilo-Saharan A.	1 — G T	R	Special language of the foreign migrants in Ghana.
41, 42.	Sotho—Tswana, *seSotho, seTswana*	SA: Lesotho, Botswana, Republic of South Africa	3.5 M + 0.9 M	D, W: Bantu G: Benue-Congo	5 — D G T S	A E P R L	Closely neighboring languages, phoneti-cally influenced by Bushman-Hottentot. Important modern literature.
43, 44.	Sukuma—Nyamwezi, *kiSukuma, kiNyamwezi*	EA: Tanganyika	0.9 + 0.4 M	D, W: Bantu G: Benue-Congo	3 — D G	E	Contiguous languages (dialects?).

No.	Language	Distribution	Speakers	Classification	6—DGTS AEPRL	Notes
45.	Swahili, *kiSwahili*	EA: Comoro Islands, Tanganyika, Zanzibar, Kenya, Somalia CA: Congo-K., Uganda, Zambia	12 to 15 M	D, W: Bantu G: Benue-Congo	6—DGTS AEPRL	The most important African language; national language of Zanzibar and Tanganyika (Tanzania); official in Kenya and Congo-**K**. Arabic and Latin transcriptions. Very abundant literature. International Committee in Dar es Salaam. Expanding.
46.	Tiv (Munshi)	WA: Sudanic-Guinean: N. Nigeria (lower Benue)	1 M	D: Nigero-Cameroonian W: Isolated class language G: Benue-Congo	3—D G · A E (until 1960)	The Tiv provoked bloody riots at independence in Nigeria to protest against the the imposition of Hausa as the national language.
47.	Umbundu (Quimbundo), *uMbundu*	SA: (W) Angola	1.5 M	D, W: Bantu G: Benue-Congo	2—D G T · ? E	
48.	Wolof (Valafe), *Wɔlɔf*	WA: Coastal Sudan; Senegal, Gambia	1.5 M	D: Senegalo-Guinean W, G: West Atlantic	2—D G · R	Lingua franca and prestige language in Senegal.
49, 50.	Yao—Makonde *ciYao, ciMakonde*	EA: Tanganyika, Mozambique, Malawi	0.5 + 0.3 + 0.15 (Neighboring languages)	D, W: Bantu G: Benue-Congo	2—G · ?	

*Indicates a group.

TABLE 1—*continued*

No.	LANGUAGE OR GROUP*	GEOGRAPHICAL ZONE	No. OF SPEAKERS	CLASSIFICATION	DOCU-MENTATION	USAGE	COMMENTS
51.	Yoruba, *Yorùbá*	Guinean WA: W. Nigeria, Dahomey, Togo	5 M +	D: Nigero-Cameroonian W: Kwa G: Kwa	5 — D G T S	A E P R L	Semiofficial in Western Nigeria; abundant literature. Lingua franca.
52.	Zande (Azande), *Pazande*	CA: Southern Sudan: Congo-K., Central African Republic	1 M	D: Ubangian W: Nigritic G: Adamawa-Eastern	3 — D G T	A E ?	Seems to have been abandoned for administrative and educational purposes in the Sudan since independence.

Map 1. — Official and National Languages of Africa

TUNISIA
MOROCCO
ALGERIA
LIBYA
SPANISH
SAHARA
UNITED
ARAB REPUBLIC
MAURITANIA
MALI
NIGER
SENEGAL
CHAD
SUDAN
GAMBIA
UPPER
VOLTA
PORT
GUINEA
GUINEA
NIGERIA
ETHIOPIA
IVORY
COAST
SIERRA
LEONE
CENTRAL
AFRICAN REPUBLIC
LIBERIA
GHANA
DAHOMEY
TOGO CAMEROON
UGANDA
SOMALIA
RIO MUNI
GABON
RUANDA
KENYA
CONGO
KINSHASA
CONGO
BRAZZAVILLE
BURUNDI
CABINDA
TANZANIA
ANGOLA
MALAWI
ZAMBIA
SOUTH-WEST
AFRICA
SOUTHERN
RHODESIA
MOZAMBIQUE
BOTSWANA
SWAZILAND
REPUBLIC
OF
SOUTH AFRICA
LESOTHO

//// Arabic

|||| French

\\\\ African languages

≡ English

} } } Afrikaans

▓ Spanish

∴∴ Portuguese

different views concerning the position of Koalib-Tagoï, but nobody else may ever understand or share these views, even if they are interested in Africa at another level. In the following chapter, which is limited to the problems of general linguistics, we must nevertheless say a word about these groups and the theoretical questions they pose.

To conclude this chapter, mention must be made of linguistic geography, or the way in which languages are distributed over the land. Here, again, much work remains to be done, largely for the reasons already given in connection with the classification of African languages. Even if we had an exact listing of languages (and dialects) in use, we would still have to answer the complicated question of *who* speaks *what, where,* and *when.* The answer lies often in recourse to sociology or anthropology (when?) as much as in geography (where?). Without entering into the details, we must not forget that the present boundaries of African states do not correspond to linguistic boundaries. This situation results not only from the fact that today's political boundaries are the heritage of last century's colonial diplomacy, which worked with a ruler and a red pencil on inaccurate maps in the quiet of European chancelleries. It also results from the lack of precision demonstrated by linguistic frontiers in Africa as they were even before European intervention. The African peasant, and even more the trader or town-dweller, is generally polyglot to a degree which western Europeans cannot easily imagine: in this sense the African situation was, if we may use the term, Balkanized long before one spoke of "Balkanization."

In one apparently paradoxical sense—but only apparently so—it is in the regions of easiest communication, those where the most important languages are localized, that multilingualism seems most highly developed. It is much less developed in those areas where transport is difficult and language heterogeneity great. The solution to this paradox obviously lies in the ease of communication. In the refugee areas, the inhabitants of one isolated community have virtually no contact except with their immediate neighbors, and one or two languages suffice for all their needs of communication. Conversely, in regions of easier contact, communication acquires greater importance, not only for economic reasons—the existence of a large radius of action—but also because these societies, which frequently have a statelike or protostate system, often attain a high degree of ethnic complexity. In economic and political systems where writing occupied little or no place, the establishment of empires or of virtually feudal-type hegemonies has necessitated the spread of one language, or sometimes two or more languages, over a wide area, without necessarily bringing about the disappearance of previously existing languages. This has been even more noticeable because diverse ethnic groups have often acquired or developed functional specializations within the whole system, thereby preserving their own culture. In this way, the large emirates of Nigeria, for example, born in Uthman Dan Fodio's Holy Wars of the early nineteenth century, call to mind the Austro-Hungarian Empire before 1914 (remember the Balkans!). In a region such as Ilorin we find, either associated or juxtaposed: Arabic, the language of prestige and religion; Fulfulde, retained by the conquering Fulani aristocracy (at least until rather recently); Hausa, the administrative language of the Sokoto empire; Yoruba, the language of the town-dwellers, who founded the city; and finally, in the surrounding countryside, the languages of peasants who have been successively subjugated by the Yoruba and the Fulani. To all this must still be added the Dyula of Mande traders and, today, English and Pidgin. Even if we admit that Islam often promotes intertribal marriages, we have here a situation in which one person in the course of his daily activities may have to use two or three languages besides his paternal and maternal languages.

We need not stress that in these conditions it becomes difficult to estimate not only the number of speakers of a given language, a figure usually greater than the number of members of that tribe to which the language properly belongs, but also the exact limits of its spread (the record has probably been set by Swahili: 15 million users at the minimum, of which only 2 million are Waswahili). Indeed, in many cases, we must speak, not of geography, but of stratigraphy: these superimpositions of languages are not easily represented on a map.

CHAPTER II

African Linguistics:
Why, What for, How?

Historical survey of linguistic research in Africa: the pioneers of the sixteenth and seventeenth centuries; decadence resulting from the slave trade; nineteenth-century antislavery and return to research; early predominance of the German school; birth of the British and French schools and internationalization of the study. "Why bother?"—an attempted reply. Theory and practice. The professor and the cleaning lady. Research methods: questionnaire, tape recorder, phonetic and phonological transcriptions. Linguistics as a vital auxiliary to other liberal-arts studies.

African linguistics—really, is there such a thing as African or Africanist linguistics? The point can be debated on the theoretical level, depending especially on whether one applies the term "linguistics" to the study of language in general or to the study of particular languages. Although I am myself a partisan of the former, I still insist on using the expression "African linguistics" to mean the particular application of methods from general linguistics to the systematic study of African languages.

African linguistics was born in the nineteenth century, shortly after the birth of general linguistics. It is not accidental that the first pioneers in the field, or the greatest among them, were primarily Germans. Obviously, some African languages had been studied before this time. At this point, I think it useful to point out that a linguist is not necessarily a polyglot, nor is a polyglot necessarily a linguist, although a knowledge of several languages may obviously be an advantage for a linguist, just as a knowledge of linguistics can help students of foreign languages.

The first important works dealing with the study of African languages by non-Africans were published in the seventeenth century by Catholic missionaries. The best known of these is a Kikongo grammar published in Rome in 1659 by Father Jacinto Brusciotto di Vetralla and titled *Regulae quaedam pro difficillimi Congensium idiomatis faciliori captu ad grammaticae normam redactae.* This study was greatly ahead of its time—although the title certainly is a period piece. What makes it even more modern, if one can use the term, is that Father Brusciotto apparently never set foot in the Congo but wrote his book on the basis of the observations, translations, and compilations of word lists set down by missionaries who were working there. Even earlier, in the late fifteenth century, some European writers had obtained West African word lists from Portuguese explorers. In this they were following the example set by Arab geographers and travelers, whose works enable us to trace certain Sudanic (West African) roots back to the tenth century. In addition, certain Islamized ethnic groups, especially the Swahili, Fulani, and Hausa, began at a very early date to write their own languages in Arabic script. The oldest works have not been preserved, but we do know that certain of them date from before the fifteenth century.

From the late seventeenth to the late eighteenth century the slave trade caused a considerable setback to a knowledge of Africa. Indeed, a scientific study of the black continent only began again hesitantly with the development of the antislavery movement, to which it is intimately connected. In a way, philanthropists and philosophers, in order to justify their humanitarian campaigns, needed to prove not only the dignity but even the basic humanity of the African. In the sixteenth century, Vittoria had attempted to do this through theological arguments; in the Age of the Enlightenment recourse was had to the rationalist arguments which laid the foundations of modern social science. In the nineteenth century, the two currents of thought began to converge in the work of missionary-explorers like Livingstone. Only after the end of World War I, however, do we see the beginning of autonomous scientific Africanist studies in the sense of the geographical specialization of various academic disciplines, based on the acquisition of fundamental knowledge of the African societies rather than on the practical satisfaction of colonial needs or religious proselytization. Thus began the study of Africa itself and for itself.

An important fact to remember is that exploratory linguistic endeavors followed two different directions, which coincided only in the late nineteenth century. The first path centered particularly on the

Cape of Good Hope and then headed northward; the second, and slightly later, began on the Atlantic Coast and then moved eastward. Variations on these currents developed soon after; but during the nineteenth century, at least, Africanists generally were either West Africanists or Bantuists—a dichotomy whose repercussions may still be felt today.

The basic unity of the Bantu languages had been suspected by the Portuguese since the seventeenth century and was rediscovered by the British at the very end of the eighteenth century. It was also demonstrated in the first half of the nineteenth century in various studies dealing with the hinterland regions of the Cape. The real foundations of Bantu studies were finally laid after 1856 by the German librarian to the Cape governor, Wilhelm Bleek, whose unfinished work, *A Comparative Grammar of South African Languages* (1862–69), introduced the very term "Bantu" into modern linguistics.

In West Africa, during the same period, another German, the missionary S. W. Koelle, was in Freetown interrogating slaves freed from slave ships by the Royal Navy. In 1854 he published *Polyglotta Africana . . . : Comparative Vocabularies of More than 100 Distinct African Languages*, which has played the same role for the languages subsequently called "Sudanic" as Bleek's *Comparative Grammar* has for the Bantu languages.

Following these two men, the German school continued to dominate the field for almost a century. Two strong personalities led this school: Carl Meinhof (d. 1944) for Bantu languages and Diedrich Westermann (d. 1954) for Sudanic and Guinean languages. Both men applied to African languages the neogrammarian techniques which had recently proved their usefulness in Indo-European and Semitic studies. Thus it was that in 1898 and 1906, respectively, Meinhof published *Grundriss einer Lautlehre der Bantusprachen* and *Grundzüge einer vergleichenden Grammatik der Bantusprachen*. In these he reconstructed the phonetics, vocabulary, and grammatical structure of Urbantu, the hypothetical ancestor of all present Bantu languages.

Westermann dealt in a more heterogeneous sphere, one more open to Asiatic and Mediterranean influences and comprising languages which differed widely among themselves. Beginning in 1911 with *Die Sudansprachen: Eine sprachvergleichende Studie*, he undertook to do for these languages what Meinhof had done for Bantu. The problem of "Sudanic" languages was nevertheless too complex to be resolved by this first synthetic endeavor, and Westermann spent the rest of his life revising and perfecting his first hypotheses, offering new syntheses in *Völkerkunde von Afrika* (1940) and *Languages of West Africa* (with M. A.

Bryan, 1952), the second volume of *The Handbook of African Languages* published by the International African Institute in London.

In South Africa and then in Great Britain the German school in turn gave birth to a daughter school, in which the great names include Alice Werner, F. W. Migeod, Ida Ward, Sir Harry Johnston, Clement Doke, and others—to name only a few of those who have died or retired. This school, more pragmatic and less theoretical than the German school from which it issued, produced exceptionally good grammars and dictionaries until, and even after, World War II. The same claim can be made by another sister school, the school of Belgian Bantuists from the Congo, who were also influenced by Meinhof and his South African disciples.

The French school had much less numerical importance. In its early days, Maurice Delafosse (d. 1926) and later Lilias Homburger (d. 1969) based their methodology on the works of Antoine Meillet. In 1911 and 1912, these two writers, each having independently criticized the works of the German school, formulated the hypothesis of the fundamental relationship between Bantu and Sudanic languages. With the publication in 1927 of his *Die westlichen Sudansprachen und ihre Beziehungen zum Bantu*, Westermann adopted this same hypothesis.

The revolution which structural and phonological theories introduced into general linguistics beginning in the 1930's quickly influenced African linguistics. In general it is these theories which have been adopted or attacked by later generations of British, American, German, Russian, and French African linguists. This brief sample is interesting in itself to the extent to which it shows the new wave of interest (a brief new wave, some claim) in African languages. Since 1945 the study and teaching of African languages have developed on a large scale, first in London and various American universities, then at Leningrad, more recently at Moscow, and, finally, in the new African universities and, since 1958, even in Paris.

People may wonder—in fact they do wonder and frequently ask me (too frequently for my taste)—what African linguists do and what it is all for.

The answer to the first of these questions is that we study African languages. This statement requires some clarification and explanation.

The study of African languages takes place at two different levels. On the first level, we choose a language with a view to determining its structure and to providing a precise, rigorous, and systematic description of it. Such a description, nevertheless, does not amount to a grammar which would permit foreigners to learn the language described. More importantly, this description forms the scientific basis from which grammars of this type can be written (which can serve speakers of the language itself as well as foreigners wishing to learn it) and from which vocabularies or dictionaries can be compiled. All this presupposes that a practical orthographic transcription has first been chosen, although this may differ widely from the orthography a linguist uses in his technical description.[1]

On the second level, the descriptions obtained by different linguists will be compared, first in order to find typological groupings (which can have an immediate practical interest for the establishment of grammars, dictionaries, etc.), then to formulate hypotheses about the relationships between these languages which lead to their classification and eventually permit a recreation of their origin.

Obviously, it is at this latter level that one has the most difficult time answering the question "What good is it?" The answer is perhaps "None." After all, one can live and prosper without knowing that French and Russian are related to each other and to Hindi and that they descend from a common hypothetical Indo-European. At first sight, the possible relationships between South African Zulu and Senegalese Wolof would seem to contribute nothing at all to Africa.

Yet, in a period when the Black Africans, regaining or discovering certain kinds of freedom, enter the international scene as new states, anything which concerns their culture or their present life obviously has a certain interest. This interest is not wholly unnecessary and dilettante —it is not art for art's sake or knowledge for its own sake. Linguistic origins are the primary and perhaps the only source of information on prehistoric African population movements. It is easy to see the uses to which this information can be put—for better or worse—in connection with the question of pan-Africanism, for example. When we think of what Nazism succeeded in building on the basis of an erroneous interpretation—obviously a more or less recognized misinterpretation— of a linguistic theory itself partly wrong and, in any case, poorly argued,[2] we can only hope that Africa will avoid entanglements in similar errors. This makes the demolition of certain dangerous myths essential, and, for that, a rigorous scientific approach provides the best method.

We have seen how, at the first level, the study of African languages

1. For example: to indicate a half-open front vowel in a language without tones, a linguist will automatically use the notation [ɛ] from the International Phonetic Alphabet; for the same vowel in a practical transcription, the simplest notation will probably be [è], which is found on the keyboards of all French typewriters.

2. Is it really necessary once again to point out that the term "Semitic" has no other meaning than a linguistic one and that the same is true for "Aryan"?

can result directly in practical applications: dictionaries, grammars, etc. The necessity or even the utility of these kinds of applications is sometimes contested today and was thought even more debatable in the past. So significant is this problem that I will return to it in a later chapter, where it will be treated in greater detail. I must, however, contradict a frequently made claim which states that any African, from the moment he learns to read and write, is automatically qualified to produce good results in the above-mentioned practices. A similarly ridiculous claim would be that my cleaning lady, a most respectable person, could, overnight, because she has lived in Paris for over a half-century, teach French at the Sorbonne or even at the local elementary school. Basically, this idea comes from the old myth about the "simplicity" and "easiness" of "primitive" languages. We are consequently surprised to see that some African students in our French universities still maintain this notion. It is unfortunately true that all too many of these students— brought up from the age of six in an educational system working uniquely with French, sent to a boarding school from the age of twelve, and living outside their country for long periods while they attend the university— partly forget their mother tongue, with tragic consequences for their re-establishment in their own country once their studies are finished.

Another explanation for this attitude comes from the general public ignorance (even the educated public) of the methods, goals, and results of the relatively new science of linguistics, which is as distinct from classical philology as from normative or prescriptive grammar. Let me add that there exists, especially in France, a certain ethnocentricity, a Western cultural egotism. Paradoxically or not, that feeling often results in universalistic, generous humanism, unfortunately founded on a regrettable confusion between the essential equality of all men and their identity. To insist on the differences, or even to point them out, is a priori suspect in the eyes of many sincere liberals—with reason, alas, in view of the distortions to which various racist ideas often subject objective, scientific observations, themselves neutral but subject to odious interpretations.

Every Frenchman—or practically all of them—believes or feels himself to be a grammarian by divine right.[3] Whether he is a conservative or a liberal, he tends to erect as universal rules the means of expression and conceptualization of his own language. I firmly believe that French teachers of all political persuasions would have approved without any alteration the *Discourse on the Universality of the French Language* by the royalist Rivarol. This same tendency has contaminated the French

3. France, to my knowledge, is the only country in the world where the great majority of popular newspapers contain a regular grammatical feature article.

Africans to the point where I myself have been accused of colonialism by a Cameroonian student for having proclaimed that there is no article in the Bantu languages. Since he was both a nationalist and a progressive, this young man accused me of having taken a racist position by refusing to recognize the existence in his language of what he believed to be a universal category in the human mind.

Among its other consequences, this misguided universalism has produced too many so-called African grammars, done by European and African amateurs, where we find the paradigms of the French language down to the last details, even including the obsolete second form of the conditional past and the pluperfect subjunctive (but not the double-compound past tense, which does exist in spoken French, although not in grammar textbooks). In brief, these writers have tried at any cost to take a normative description of French (usually grossly incorrect) and to force into this framework the particular structures and forms of the African languages which they thought they were describing and even regulating. But the golden rule in modern linguistic description is, quite to the contrary, that each language constitutes a system which can be described only in reference to itself, with particular attention given to avoiding the pitfalls of translation.[4]

A simple concrete example should enable the reader to understand quickly what this rule actually means, for it may seem a bit abstract. Take the following Swahili sentence:

Ali akaa hapa,

to which we juxtapose a word-by-word translation, completely identical at first sight:

Ali akaa hapa.
Ali lives here.

The pitfall into which certain recent works have fallen is to propose the following reasoning: *hapa* = "here." "Here" is a locative adverb. Thus *hapa* = locative adverb. The initial mistake is the equation *hapa* = "here." What should be said is: "In this Swahili sentence, *hapa* is translated into English by the adverb 'here.'" Nothing else.

Indeed, to say that "here" is in English a locative adverb is to say that this word may play the same role in a sentence as a whole series of other words or phrases which are strictly comparable with it by their

4. To teach a foreign language, it may be necessary or advantageous to refer to comparisons between certain features of the language of instruction and those of the language being taught or even to base the course on the structure of the language of instruction (although many experts currently debate this). But comparison is not assimilation.

functional behavior (e.g., "there," "behind," "far away," etc.), this series constituting a subsystem in the general system of English, a subsystem to which we may then legitimately give a tag "locative adverb," taking into account, among other things, its semantic content ("position in space").

We might have found that in Swahili *hapa* belongs to a subsystem exactly comparable with that of "here" in English, in which case we would have been correct in labeling it a "locative adverb." Such is not the case. *Hapa* does belong to a subsystem, but one composed of fourteen elements—and *only* fourteen—each having an analogous phonic structure whose role is to serve either as a substitute or as a determinant of nouns, nouns whose own particular structure in each case determines the choice among the fourteen elements of the subsystem. By proceeding to systematic comparisons of form and function *within the Swahili system* (and not in English translations), we are able to define the subsystem to which *hapa* belongs as including only determinative nominal substitutes, dependent nominals with a selective function. In this case, and only in this case, can we call them, for instance, "demonstratives," keeping well in mind that we are talking only about a label with a relative value and in no case about a total assimilation with the "demonstratives" of the English system. Obviously, these comments hold equally true for the choice of the term "noun," which I have used above and which in Swahili has its own significance, quite different from the English "noun."

Basing themselves on the principle of describing linguistic systems only in reference to themselves, some modern American writers have followed Bloomfield in affirming that it is useless, if not harmful, to know a language in order to analyze and describe it. Everything depends on what we understand by "knowing" a language. Indeed, it is not necessary to speak a language fluently or to understand it completely before proceeding to a sufficiently precise and detailed analysis which provides an acceptable general description. I myself believe, and will so do until proven wrong (which no one has yet done), that it is impossible to proceed to a satisfactory analysis before having at least an approximate understanding[5] of the notional or semantic content of a language and of the messages to analyze. Without this it is impossible to go beyond the phonic system of the language one is studying. This poses problems for the method of investigation, of which we can give only a very general idea here.

In cases where the researcher has neither an interpreter nor a common

5. In a way, all translations are necessarily only approximate and represent only an adaptation.

language with his informant, he must at least use the method of panto-mime and of pointing to objects, accompanied by appropriate sonorous emissions. This was Robinson Crusoe's method with Friday, and it is often used today by the space-, cosmo-, or astronauts when they meet up with Venusians, Martians, or other extraterrestrial creatures (the reader is asked to consult his favorite science-fiction books). This stage has generally been bypassed in present-day Africa, where, on the other hand, it is often indispensable to use an interpreter or a third language. One finds increasingly, however, that the informant has a certain knowl-edge of French or English. This greatly simplifies the linguist's task, but it also presents the risk of ridiculous errors.[6]

The experience gained over the last hundred years means that the researcher generally knows what he is looking for and often even has a rather precise idea of what he can expect to find (because of premature overconfidence, this approach may even lead to mistakes). On the prac-tical side, this means that the whole first part of the investigation is done with the help of a skeletal questionnaire, in which form and content vary according to the type of language being handled.[7] The investigator, armed with a tape recorder, a notebook, and a pen, translates a series of words and expressions, repeating them out loud until his informant is satisfied with his pronunciation before noting them in phonetic tran-scription.

Here I must open a technical parenthesis concerning the passage from *phonetic* transcription to *phonological* transcription, a crucial distinction but often elusive for the nonlinguists, who frequently find it difficult to realize that extraordinary powers of hearing can lead an observer to make incorrect notations or, more exactly, redundant notations. One can say that, generally, a phoneme is an abstraction, definable as the ensemble of pertinent characteristics which enable one basic sound of a language to be distinguished from all other sounds of that language. All these distinctions taken together make possible the structuring and the communication of the spoken information. Some concrete examples will help to clarify this notion, which is essential in modern linguistics.

6. In a vocabulary list collected in North Togo, I have found a verb *tiraku* glossed as "to have sexual relations." I suppose that on the other side of the border, in the British-administered Togoland, *tiraku* would become *fəki* or *s(i)k(u)ru*. And on an old map of Gabon a collection of rivers is called "Silo," "Dilo," "Sidilo" as a result of replies in the guide's pidgin French to the Frenchman's question "What is that?" about the topography. It was, in effect, water (*C'est de l'eau* = "That is water").

7. The current tendency is to use standardized questionnaires which permit researchers of different nationalities to make easier comparisons of collected materials. French research teams thus use questionnaires adapted from those perfected in Great Britain and the United States.

(a) The initial sound of the French word "cas" is not identical to that of "cou"; in "cas," phonetically noted [ka],[8] articulation is made in the front part of the mouth, while in "cou" [qu] it is made in the back. Nevertheless, the sounds noted, [k] and [q], are, in French, variations on a single *phoneme*, noted /k/, for there is no situation where two words with different meanings are distinguished from each other solely by either posterior or anterior articulation. In Arabic, on the contrary, ﻕ, *qâf* (the [q] of French "cou"), and ﻙ, *kaf* (the [k] of "cas"), are two separate phonemes, /q/ and /k/; that is to say, pairs of words like /kabasa/, "to lay siege to," and /qabasa/, "to ask for a light," are distinguished only by this difference in articulation.

(b) "Peach" and "beach" have quite different meanings in English. Phonemically they are distinguished only by the fact that the initial labial stop is voiceless in /pic/ and voiced in /bic/. In Alsatian German, however, this distinction does not operate on initial position—which explains the bewilderment of a whole classroom of Nawdemba school-boys when an earnest and choleric Alsatian schoolmaster thundered at them "Not 'p' as in 'peach,' you pheppering itiots, 'p' as in 'peach.'" Which was all the more confusing, since the Nawdemba live 200 miles away from the nearest beach and 2,000 miles away from the nearest peach.

Similarly, Spanish has no meaningful distinction between /s/ and /z/ in intervocalic position; people pronounce either [rosa] or [roza] for "rose" according to provincial origin or personal habit. In French, however, the distinction is meaningful, and it would not do for an enamored Spaniard to call a French girl [ros], "hag," when meaning [roz], "rose."

(c) It follows logically that it is useless to have two different signs in French to symbolize the different articulatory gymnastics of "cas" and "cou," since /k/ is a single phoneme. In Spanish it is equally useless to use two different symbols for the voiced and voiceless realizations of /s/—which one could equally well transcribe by the single symbol [z] if it were not used elsewhere. In Arabic, however, ﻙ and ﻕ differ significantly, and their notation necessitates two symbols.

I hope that these explanations, however brief and succinct, suffice to make the principle of phonological transcription meaningful: the point is to notate *not* all the possible variations of every phoneme (which would in any case be almost impossible) but rather to retain enough symbols to represent all the pertinent dichotomies in the language—and only those. This still poses certain problems, but these have no place

8. By international agreement, the phonetic notations are transcribed between brackets: [k]; phonological notations between slashes: /k/.

here. Let us simply say that a phonological (or phonemic) notation would avoid uselessly picturesque spellings such as "Conakry" (why not "Konakri"?) or "N'Krumah" with an apostrophe (a French habit; he himself writes "Nkrumah").

After establishing the phonological system of the language and setting down the guidelines for general rules which govern the phonetic realities, the researcher may turn to the grammar and syntax by proceeding to the systematic transposition of elements between the parts of the utterance which he will already have transcribed during the first investigation. This consists, for example, in beginning with a sentence like "The child saw the pretty horse" and first substituting words like "the woman," "the dog," and "the policeman," for "the child" and then, for "horse," substituting "cow," "house," "piano," and so on. Here, again, I cannot go into detail, but the reader will easily guess the difficulties which may arise from a careless application of the method. One might, for instance, propose to the informant an exchange of the kind "The flower ate the brave piano."

At this stage of the investigation, a trained linguist can already sketch an outline of the general characteristics of the language he is studying. Before his study can be reasonably complete, the researcher must collect texts *in vivo* and no longer *in vitro*: first, fables and narratives, which are analyzed word by word, and then—and herein lies the great progress made possible by the invention of the tape recorder—conversations of all kinds, which one may call free conversation or living speech. After all this, prudence should counsel the researcher to write up his synthesis and to publish his study in a form which permits the native speakers themselves to continue the work. Failing this, the researcher runs the risk of letting himself go further and further with microspecialization, which may lead him to consecrate his whole life to a language form used by 600, 6,000, or 600,000 speakers—which may certainly be exciting for him (and may bring him academic renown) but which will constitute no less certainly a waste of time and effort in the present state of Africa's needs.

The steps outlined above constitute a fairly reasonable way of serving an apprenticeship in a language while penetrating the culture which the language expresses. The British school (correctly, I think)[9] regards the linguistic investigation as being an indispensable prerequisite for any intensive anthropological investigation. In the United States a linguist such as Sapir was also a great anthropologist, and an anthropologist such as Boas was an excellent linguist. Today, however, increasing specialization tends—if only because of the enormous volume of

9. I may as well admit it now: I have my degree from London.

literature to keep up with—to a decrease in the number of well-rounded or "general" anthropologists. Any analysis in depth of a civilization nevertheless requires some knowledge of the language. A linguistic training is consequently indispensable for the anthropologist. The reverse is not necessarily true, although the linguist in the field must be at least a bit of an anthropologist. Thus was born ethnolinguistics, a field sometimes looked upon as a bit of a bastard child and which is still in the process of finding itself. The present rehabilitation of African cultures promises a definite future for it.

The same holds true for certain branches of applied linguistics which, in the realms of pedagogy and mass communication, for example, require sociological and psychological as well as linguistic knowledge. We will return to this when treating these problems specifically.

CHAPTER III

Surely No One Speaks an African Language, Do They?

(A) General characteristics of African languages: some old wives' tales. The poverty of African languages: a myth! The absence of abstract ideas in African languages: a myth! The absence of grammar: another myth. Truly unique or peculiar characteristics: (1) phonetic traits: clicks; other special phonemes; (2) tone; (3) morphology: classes; (4) ideophones or impressives; (5) reduplication and repetition.

(B) Presentation of several major languages: class languages: Bantu (Swahili, Bulu), West Atlantic (Fulfulde). Languages without classes: Hamito-Semitic family (Hausa), Kwa group (Yoruba), Mande group (Mandinka, Susu), Nilo-Saharan family (Songhaï). Trade languages: Pidgin, Kriyol.

(C) Classification of African languages: methodological overview; usefulness of genetic classification. Results, hypotheses, and theories: classifications by Delafosse, by Westermann and the London School, and by Greenberg.

Obviously it is virtually impossible to give a detailed presentation of the results of more than a century of in-depth research concerning more than one hundred languages (the others having been only vaguely reconnoitered). In this chapter we shall limit ourselves to a sketch—with supporting examples—of the typology of the most important ones. Then we shall present and briefly discuss the different genetic classifications proposed by the French, Anglo-German, and American schools.

Before moving on to the proposed description, however, I think I should mention several special or general characteristics of African languages. Remember that I am only concerned with languages spoken to the south of a line which follows the southern edge of the Sahara from the Atlantic Ocean and joins the Indian Ocean near the southern frontier of Somalia. (North of this line most of the languages belong to a family considered "classic," in the sense that some of the languages belonging to it have been written for centuries and are Afro-Asiatic [to borrow J. Greenberg's expression] rather than African. These languages have long been studied and described as much by European philologists as by local grammarians. Arabic and Ge'ez, or classical Ethiopian, are excellent examples of this.) Moreover, the geographic region the African languages cover corresponds only vaguely with what we call Black Africa. The limits of Black Africa are neither absolute nor always very precise. At the end of this chapter I shall try to place these languages on a general map of the African linguistic situation, although to do this I shall have to make an exception—which is debatable but important— to the very rule which I have just established.

I have already outlined the general characteristics of African languages. The first which I shall discuss might be called the negative characteristics; more precisely, I must explode some widespread myths.

The first myth to explode: "*African languages are poor.*" Certain scholars who should know better (sometimes they even hold M.A.'s or Ph.D.'s), continue to say that "these dialects include only a few hundred —or a few thousand—words." This presumes first of all that they have an answer to a problem in general linguistics which is quite far from being solved: the nature of a "word." Even if one concedes, as one might easily do, that a word is a linguistic unit which deserves a separate entry or a separate article in a dictionary, it would still be difficult to determine what constitutes the wealth of a language. Does it involve the total number of words in a dictionary? If this is the case, then written languages have an advantage from the start: that of lexical sedimentation, which writing permits. If I flip through my dictionary at random, I will find many words that I will never use or will use only rarely, such as "deictic," "hexadichloroethane," "gules," "modulus," "parbuckle," and "certiorari." It might indeed seem that we should admit that the vocabulary which people possess, given an equal intellectual capacity of the speakers, is practically identical from one language to another and that where we speak of a language used in a technologically complex civilization we should speak of different specialized dialects, mutually incomprehensible between different professional categories.

African languages may seem poor if one examines the few published lexicons. This so-called poverty stems directly from the lexicographers' ignorance of the language they were studying or of the civilization these languages expressed—and sometimes, too, from an ignorance, if not of their own language, at least of the language in which they wrote. Despite these obstacles, dictionaries do exist whose size compares well with that of the *American Heritage Dictionary, Webster's Collegiate, Chambers,* or the abridged *O.E.D.* Examples include, among others, the Mande dictionary by Delafosse, the Hausa ones by Bargery or Abraham, the Swahili dictionaries of Sacleux, Krapf, or Madan, and the Kongo dictionaries by Laman or Bentley.

One last point: it seems probable that in civilizations whose culture is exclusively or primarily oral, the active vocabulary[1] which each person has at his command is larger—precisely because of the lack of graphic memory aids—than it is in a civilization which makes extensive use of writing.

Second myth to explode: "African languages have a fundamentally concrete orientation and do not lend themselves to expression of abstract ideas." This myth is an offshoot of the former one and belongs to the same general category of misunderstandings about African civilizations. Without specific changes, no language can ever express more than the total context in which it is used. Notice the word *total.* This is self-evident for the material context: there is obviously no English word meaning "hippopotamus" (we use a Greek word) or "kangaroo" (the word is based on a misunderstanding on the part of the earliest explorers). We can as readily concede that a language of Equatorial Africa will have no word for "apple tree" or "snowdrift"; but as soon as so-called abstract terms enter in, a European or American, applying a kind of scholasticism of universals, whether consciously or not, is astonished at not being able to translate word for word certain ideas which seem to him not only natural but universal. It happens that "abstract" terms are those which belong to a nonmaterial context: to the values of a civilization or, in the final analysis, to a system of relations which forms the structure of this civilization. Basically this opposition of *concrete* to *abstract* is not quite satisfactory. It would probably be better to use terms such as *substantial* and *relational.* Surely an African living in a civilization different from our own must regard French or English as being singularly lacking in abstract terms. To prove this, it suffices to read modern ethnographic works: almost invariably the authors must retain the African terms, or give a long

---

1. Active vocabulary: one which is actually used or spoken as opposed to a vocabulary which is merely understood. The passive vocabulary is always larger than the active vocabulary where literacy is widespread.

definition, often complex and only approximate, the first time they use an African word. At another level, a lexicographer can easily collect terms designating visible, tangible objects in the physical setting, such as parts of the human body, common tools, furniture, etc., precisely because he can show them or touch them. But what of an idea such as the "acquisition of a moral and economic preponderance at the expense of someone else thanks to the possession of an evil supernatural substance held in lawful bounds by the presence of vital energy with a cosmic origin" (in Bulu, *asée*)?

The argument has been even more convincingly set forth as the incapacity to extract the common denominator from a series of objects or analogous beings by arguing, for instance, that some languages have a term to indicate every species and variety of antelope but no word for antelope in general. Similarly, on a French boat one finds hawsers, sheets, halyards, bowlines, sluices, gaskets, etc. but no rope—which proves that French sailors are incapable of abstraction. Here again it really comes down to a cultural difference. There is no inability to abstract (in the strict sense of the word: "pull out of") but only different means of abstracting wherein the criteria are not identical. Thus some people have maintained that Africans cannot distinguish more than three colors—black, white, and red—a conclusion based on an overly rapid analysis of their languages. What seems really to happen is that the chromatic terminology of these languages is based more on vividness than on shades: "red" would be, approximately, "vivid"; "white" is "clear" or "pale"; "black" is "somber" or "lofty"—the shades being suggested by reference to objects (as we do with "orange"). What is involved, in brief, is the expression of different world views, which are, however, no less complete or complex. A language may be more analytical in some spheres, more synthetic in others. The global wealth of expression may well be the same for all languages.

One last argument: "*In African languages there are no words for hypotenuse, plesiosaurus, circumference, and ontology.*" Response: Nor are there any in French or in English. I will come back to this question of scientific vocabulary later.

Third myth to be exploded: African languages are (a) *very easy,* (b) *very difficult, because they have no grammar.*" There is no language without grammar. At least not in this world.

Now that we have thus summarily disposed of some wrong ideas, let us turn to some more or less positive aspects—none of which constitutes an absolute—of the languages we shall examine.

1. On the phonetic and phonological level, we should first point out

an African monopoly: the *clicks*, which, to put it technically, are implosive, injective consonants with double articulation. The uninitiated reader can get some idea of the corresponding sound by making the following approximate comparisons: the labial click, written ⊙, recalls a mother's kiss for a baby; the alveolar clicks, written as / and ϕ, recall the disapproving sound "tut-tut"; palatoalveolar clicks, written ! and ≠, recall some tongue-cluckings made by mule skinners. As for lateral clicks, written /// and // (sometimes *x*), only one comparison comes to mind: someone cleaning his teeth loudly with his tongue. In French or English, then, all of these sounds are only *noises* and do not enter into the phonological system of the language; but let us insist that in Africa they are used as phonemic consonants which serve to form syllables. I suggest the following exercise for those who wish to give themselves an idea of the pronunciation difficulties this represents. Say [*ba*] or [*pa*], then try to repeat it by replacing [*b*] or [*p*] by ⊙ and continue on in the same way with [*ta*] > [/*a*], etc. (I advise against performing these exercises in front of a group which has not been warned in advance.) Next, one might go on to aspirated, prenasalized, and other combinations. I must admit that these phonemes have a limited geographic spread. Originally restricted to the languages of the Bushmen and Hottentots of South Africa (and to the two related groups in East Africa, the Sandawe and the Hadza), they have penetrated only the neighboring Bantu languages (i.e., the Nguni and Sotho-Tswana groups).

Much more frequently found are labiovelar phonemes, which are extremely rare outside of Black Africa. The three most widespread are generally noted as [*kp*], [*gb*], and [*ŋm*], transcriptions which give only an approximate idea of their pronunciation. These are found in West and Central Africa from Guinea to the Upper Nile. Also frequently found are injective and implosive consonants, pronounced with a rush of air which is not followed by an immediate relaxation of the organs (an approximate English example: the [*p*] in "stop").[2]

One other point must be noted: the great, indeed almost universal, frequency of prenasalized consonants, semioccluded nasals, and complexes with syllabic consonants [*mb*, *nd*, *ng*, etc.], which have resulted in "Frafrican" spellings such as "N'Krumah," "N'Zerekore," "N'Gaoundere," etc.

2. The question of tones deserves special mention. Most African languages are languages with significant tones. The musical pitch of one

---

2. I do not propose here to enter into the technical details of the articulatory phonetics which fall outside the general framework of the book. To the interested reader I recommend the classical work by Ida Ward and Diedrich Westermann *Practical Phonetics for the Students of African Languages* (London, 1933).

syllable is as important to the meaning of the message as the timbre of the vowels or the articulation of the consonants. Unlike the tonal languages of Southeast Asia, the major contrast comes from the relative height of each tone in relationship to the others rather than from their melodic shape (rising, falling, level). Many tones may be heard as contoured—rising or falling—but this is usually only the effect of a passage from high to low or the reverse.

Europeans, and particularly the French, are accustomed to a language where pitch plays no phonemic role and where intonation, especially expressing humor or emotion, is extremely flexible. They have spent a long time discovering the existence and particularly the role of tones. Yet their role is critical, sometimes more significant than the role of the vowel timbres. In fact, tones not only serve to differentiate lexemes ("words") which are absolutely homonymous from all other viewpoints, but they also allow the functioning of grammatical or syntactical mechanisms such as the verbal conjugation, the relationships of nominal nexus ("genitive"), and so forth. Some examples borrowed from Bulu, a Bantu language of the Cameroon, will provide explicit illustration of this.

Bulu has two basic tones, high /´/ and low /`/, and these may be combined in composite tones, ascending /ˇ/ and descending /ˆ/.[3] First we shall look at pairs of words:

àbè = "thigh"		*àbé* = "breast"	
m̀bàŋ = "elephant tusk"		*m̀bàŋ́* = "palm nut"	
má^ʔán = "payment"		*mà^ʔàn* = "crossroads"	
kɔ̀è = "monkey"		*kɔ́é* = "snail"	
—*kàt* = "to say"		—*kát* = "to fail"	

There are many other such examples of words that are distinguished only by their tone—with the possibility of grotesque confusion, as one might guess. (There is an Ntumu village where I have only to show my face to set off a wild general laughter, more than ten years after committing an error of this kind.)

In the same language, tone has a determining role in conjugation, either for differentiating tenses:

à-ŋgà-yèm   "He is beginning to know."
à-ŋgá-yêm   "He knew, he has known."
à-ŋgá-yèm   "He will know one day."

---

3. The usual practice is not to note one of the basic tones, usually the low one, since it is the *high:low* opposition which is relevant. Here I have noted both in order to be more explicit.

or for making the verb agree with its subject:

bì-kèyâ	"We left."
bí-kèyâ	"They (e.g., *bìvét*, "the chiefs") left."
mì-á-bɔ̀	"You do."
mí-á-bɔ̀	"They (e.g., *mìntáŋán*, "the whites") do."

I could give many more examples of this sort with different facts but always ending in the same result: it is impossible to speak, or rather to communicate, without respecting the tones, especially in languages where monosyllabic vocables and morphemes (grammatical operators) predominate. Nevertheless, it is only recently that tonal studies, begun in the late nineteenth century by the Germans, have taken a front seat in the works of Africanists. Given the present state of these works, it seems necessary to distinguish basically between systems with two registers (high and low) and systems with three registers (high, medium, and low). Other researchers have postulated a different system: an original and unique system of two levels, to which one could reduce all those which at first sight look more complex. Basically, the question has barely been touched, and much more research is necessary in both the laboratory and the field before we can give a solidly grounded answer.

3. The *morphological* complexity varies widely: one finds as many languages where the syntactical and grammatical markers are reduced to variations of position and of tone, with a very small number of morphemes or functional monemes, as one finds languages where, on the contrary, such morphemes abound and are combined with tonal variations and positional constraints.

Most languages with complex morphologies are *class languages*, of which Bantu is the most characteristic. The great majority of modern linguists believe that classes are essentially grammatical categories, schemes of agreement, comparable, from certain viewpoints, to Latin declensions or to German genders (among others). Certain linguists nevertheless contend that classes have a primarily semantic value and correspond to an attempt at separating objects and beings into categories, each one of which corresponds to a general idea: "human beings," "vegetables," "liquids," "body parts," "animals," etc.[4]

In my opinion, classes most frequently have both a grammatical *and* a semantic value, although there is no absolute correspondence between the two.

---

4. Interestingly enough, the main supporters of this second theory are often the same people who refuse to admit that Africans have the gift of abstraction and synthesis.

At the beginning of the century many Africanists saw class languages as an archaic type, viewing the existence of classes as a result of the so-called "primitive mentality." More recent works, however, indicate that class languages are of a relatively recent nature, probably having developed from languages without classes (whereas in 1900 it was thought that these latter had lost their classes through evolution). The question remains an open one, and there is no guarantee that it will ever be definitely answered.

4. Another widespread characteristic in all of Black Africa (and one which spread even into Madagascar) is the existence of a category of vocables baptized with various names: "descriptive adverbs," "exclamatory descriptions," "predicative interjections," "impressives," "image words," or "ideophones." The wealth of these names indicates the prevailing uncertainty about their exact nature. I personally prefer the terms "ideophones" (by analogy to "ideograms") and "impressives," for the closest definition one can give for them is approximately "vocables which transmit a sensorial feeling or a complex moral emotion." Some of these are onomatopoetic, like "boom, boom" or "rat-a-tat," evoking the feeling produced by some act or incident through the noise which accompanies it. This is, however, only a special case, and the etymology of most others remains a mystery, unless it involves a kind of synesthesia which escapes us. Examples include:

Bulu: *ne viú*,   "feeling of almost total darkness or of a very heavy shadow"

   ne véta,   "feeling of fatigue, especially mental, of lassitude after an intellectual effort"

Ewe: *lílílí*,   "the impression of a pleasant odor"

   lìlìlì,   "the impression of a bad odor"

Swahili: *ndi*,   "the impression of moral or physical fixity"

   koco,   "the impression of abundance, of profusion"

5. Finally, the reduplication of a vocable, of its root, or of a part of its root is a very common trait; its function may be stylistic, semantic, or grammatical:

STYLISTIC: Swahili: *nyungu imevunjika vipande vipande*,   "The pot is broken into a thousand pieces" (literally, "pieces, pieces").

SEMANTIC: Ganda: *bafumba*,   "They are cooking."

   bafumbafumba,   "They are playing at cooking, pretending to cook."

GRAMMATICAL: Hausa: *múúní,* "ugliness"
                    mummúúnáá, "ugly"

I shall now present a sample of various major languages which belong to different groups. These are not necessarily the most typical of each group—Swahili, for example, is one of the rare nontonal Bantu languages—but are rather the most widely spoken and the best known (by which I mean known to European linguists). Where a standard transcription exists, I have used it for the text. The detailed glosses have been phonologically transcribed wherever possible.

Some of the sample texts were chosen and explained by several of my colleagues, to whom I again express my thanks:

Fulfulde and Songhaï: Professor Pierre F. Lacroix, Ecole des Langues Orientales.
Hausa: Professor Claude Gouffé, Ecole des Langues Orientales.
Yoruba: Professor Robert F. Armstrong, University of Ibadan.
Mandinka and Susu: Dr. Maurice Houis, IFAN, University of Dakar.

I have deliberately left each of these scholars free to choose the format of his presentation, so as to give the reader a more varied methodological sampling.

1. CLASS LANGUAGES: BANTU

The system of noun classes, characteristic of a large proportion of African languages, reaches its maximum development in the Bantu languages. The first language given as an example, Swahili, is not completely typical in that, first, it is not a tonal language and, second, its vocabulary includes a large number of Arabic loanwords; even the name "Swahili" comes from the Arabic *sahil,* "coast" (here, the Indian Ocean coast). Nevertheless, the grammatical structures are typically Bantu; and since Swahili is the largest language in Black Africa, spoken from the Comoros to the Congo, it is important to give some idea of this language.

Classes are grammatical categories, patterns of agreement, marked in Bantu by characteristic prefixes. The choice of patterns of agreement, that is, the choice of characteristic prefixes for the words that agree, is ruled by the grammatical substantive subject of the utterance, from which comes the name "noun classes." The following are two examples of such patterns:

1   *mtu m̲kubwa y̲ule a̲meanguka*
    man   large   this   is-fallen

7   *kitu k̲ikubwa k̲ile k̲imeanguka.*
    thing   large   this   is-fallen

Here *mtu* and *kitu* are the substantives (nouns)—or *Independent Nominals* (IN)[5]—governing the agreement between pronoun-adjectives (= dependent nominals, dn), *-kubwa* and *-le*, and of the verb (Vb) *-anguka* through the underlined prefixes. All the IN which govern the same agreement as *mtu* form a class; all those which govern the same agreement as *kitu* form another class, and so on. Bantuists have set up twenty-one such patterns for the whole of the Bantu domain, generally numbered in the order of their discovery.

Let us now add two more examples to those which have just been analyzed:

2   *watu wakubwa wale wameanguka*
    men   large   these   are-fallen

8   *vitu   vikubwa   vile   vimeanguka*
    things   large   these   have-fallen

The reader will immediately notice that these are in the relationship of *singular:plural* opposition, with reference to the first examples. The conclusion to be drawn is that in Swahili (as in most Bantu languages), the IN of class 1 form their plural in class 2, while those of class 7 form theirs in class 8. We may thus say that *grammatical genders* exist for the two classes 1/2 and 7/8.

Let us return to the four IN subjects of our utterances: *mtu, watu, kitu,* and *vitu*. The reader will immediately notice that they have a structure identical to that of the dn: *mkubwa, wakubwa, kikubwa, vikubwa,* and *yale, wale, kile, vale*—that is, a fixed element, *-tu,* the *root* or *stem,* and a variable prefix, *m-, wa-, ki-, vi-*. There nevertheless exists an important semantic difference: while *-kubwa* and *-le* keep the same meaning ("large" and "this") irrespective of the prefix attached to them, with which they harmonize, the meaning "man" may, however, *only* be attached to the pair *mtu/watu* and the meaning "thing" *only* to the pair *kitu/vitu*. What is more, a systematic investigation will reveal that the root *-tu* can take on only these four prefixes—1, 2, 7, and 8—while *-kubwa* and *-le* can take on any prefixes in the language. This is the difference which constitutes the criterion of distinction between

5. Terminology specifically conceived for Bantu languages by the London School.

the IN and the dn, the latter being called "dependents" precisely because the choice of their prefix depends on the class of the Independent Nominal subject of the utterance (*nomen regens*).

Two IN may be in a relationship of dependence of the second in relationship to the first (genitive or noun complement); this relationship is marked by the addition to the noun (IN) ruled by an *extradependent prefix* (edp), which plays the same role as the simple *dependent prefix* (dp) of the dependent nominals.

$_8vitu$	$_8vya$	$_1mtu$	"the things of the man"
$_8vitu$	$_8vya$	$_2watu$	"the things of men"
$_2watu$	$_2wa$	$_8vitu$	"the men of things"[6]

If we next consider the last word from the first examples, its verbal element, we will observe a series of prefix alternations which are analogous (but not formally identical) to those of the dn: there is one apparently fixed element, *-meanguka*, and four variable prefixes, *a-, wa-, ki-, vi-*. Does this mean that *-meanguka* is structurally identical to a dn such as *-kubwa*, for example? No. A series of permutations is going to appear in forms such as

alianguka	*ataanguka*	*haanguki*	*anguke*	etc.
he fell	he will fall	he doesn't fall	let him fall	etc.

which allow us to extract a root *-anguk-*, to which we may give the meaning "to fall," and, in addition to the class prefixes previously noted, a series of other affixes—preprefix *h(a)-*; infixes *-li-, -ta-, -ϕ-*; and suffixes *-i, -e*—which act as verbal operators specifying the different tenses of the conjugation.

And that is not all. A series of analogous commutations applied to the root will reveal that this root is a complex and belongs to a system

-ang-	*-ang-am-*	*-ang-u-*	*-ang-u-liw-*
"to float in the air"	"to be hanging in the air"	"to make fall"	"to be thrown down"

-ang-u-k-i-	*-ang-u-sh-*
"to fall in, on"	"to throw down"

This means that, beginning with a *simple or primitive root*, *-ang-*, "to be in the air," one obtains a whole series of *derived verbs*, through *infixes of derivation* or *radical extensions* (Examples 1, 2, and 3) inserted between the primitive root and the grammatical suffixes.

6. This is not a fictional example: I found the expression used to mean "materialists."

Other elements of a pronominal nature agree in class with the IN which they represent and may also infix themselves between the root and the first grammatical operator, leading to forms such as (₇*kitabu*) *kilichonisomewa*, "(₇the book) which was read to me" ("which to me was read"), which decomposes into:

1	2	3	4	5	6	7	8
ki-	*-li-*	*-cho-*	*-ni-*	*-som-*	*-e-*	*-w-*	*-a*
verbal	1st	relative	object	simple	exten-	exten-	2nd aspect,
prefix	aspect	infix,	infix,	root	sion 1,	sion 2,	grammatical
subject	past	cl. 7	cl. 1,		applica-	passive	suffix
			1st per-		tive		
			son sing.				

which gives some idea of the possibilities of agglutinative formations in Swahili (which are, however, less developed than those of other Bantu languages, such as Zulu, for example).

Obviously, it is impossible to give more than a sketch of the grammar of any one language, let alone of an entire family. I will thus limit myself to mentioning several more general or quasi-general traits of the Bantu languages, with Swahili examples.

1. First, the existence of words which do not control class agreements, are not controlled by such agreements, and cannot be decomposed into root (radical) and affixes. I call these *autonomous particles*. They are particularly frequent in Swahili, and many come from Arabic:

> *au,* "or"   *wala,* "neither"   *tu,* "only"   etc.

2. The existence of a locative, formed sometimes by prefixation as an extra-independent prefix (EIP), and sometimes, as in Swahili, by suffixation of a nonautonomous particle, which results in changing the class of the IN to which the particle is attached:

> ₉*nyumba*   ₉*i*₉(*n*)*zuri*   "The house is pretty."
> house   is-pretty

> ₁₆*nyumbani*   *ni*₁₆*pazuri*   "It feels nice in the house."
> in-the-house   it-is-nice

In the second example, the fact that *nyumba* belongs to class 9 (IP: *ny-*; dp: *i-*, *n-*) is somewhat neutralized by the locative suffix *-ni.* In certain neighboring languages one would have, with EIP 16, *panyumba* instead of *nyumbani.*

3. These two examples of locatives include *no verb.* These are some examples of nominal predication, a very widespread trait in Bantu: the

verb is replaced by an actualizer, the pre-prefix 9 *i-* in the first example (*nyumba i(n)zuri*), the prefixed nonautonomous particle *ni-* (not to be confused with the locative suffix *-ni!*) in the second example (*nipazuri*).

4. It is often possible to form nominal *diminutives* or *augmentatives* by a change of class, sometimes with a modification of the root (reduplication of the first syllable or addition of a neutral syllable). For example:

3/4, *mfuko/mifuko,* "bag, bags"   7/8, *kifuko/vifuko,* "small bag(s)"
5/6, *fuko/mafuko,* "large bag(s)"

5. Peculiarities of the class system: in Swahili the rules of class agreement have one important exception: the names of animated beings govern the agreement in class 1, no matter what their formal and etymological class may be:

Class 1	*mtu mdogo*	"small man"
Class 7	*kitabu kidogo*	"small book," but
	kiboko mdogo	"small hippopotamus"
Class 9	*nyumba ndogo*	"small house," but
	nyoka mdogo	"small snake"

This replacement of the purely grammatical agreement by a notional agreement, setting *animate* against *inanimate*, is found in several modern lingua francas based on Bantu.

6. I have stated above that a pair of classes in the oppositional relationship *singular:plural* constitutes a *gender*. But any given class may correspond to the singular of one gender and the plural of another. There is no example of this in Swahili, but in Bulu there is a gender 5/6 *alú/melú,* "night/nights," opposed to a gender 11/5 *onɔń/anɔń,* "bird/ birds."

There are also genders with a single class, sometimes called "collective genders" because they do not have the *singular:plural* opposition (particularly names of liquids, with the single class 6), and, more rarely, there are genders with three classes, most frequently in the opposition of *singular:enumerative plural:nonenumerative plural.*

7. Not all the Bantu languages have these characteristics to the same degree. Also, there are certain non-Bantu languages which have a structure closely resembling what I have sketched out above. The criteria for belonging to the Bantu group, according to Guthrie, are, on the one hand, the existence of a regular system of nominal classes and, on the other hand, the presence, in the vocabulary of a given language, of a relatively high percentage of words which may be linked by regular

sound shifts to a catalogue of common roots (Common Bantu, CB), which presently amounts to about 3,000 articles. Examples are:

CB *-ána*, "child"; Swahili: *mwana*; Kongo: *mwána*; Sotho: *ŋwána*; Bulu: *mɔ́n*; etc.

CB *-óka*, "snake"; Swahili: *nyoka*; Kongo: *nyóka*; Sotho: *nóha*; Bulu: *nyɔ́*; etc.

These are simple and obvious examples, deliberately chosen from geographically noncontiguous languages.

For the past forty years, various people have attempted with various degrees of success to reconstitute the ancestor roots common to Bantu and the other Black African languages. The most recent works of Greenberg lead one to hope for progress in this attempt in the near future.

SWAHILI TEXT

Hapo   kale   paka   hakukaa   katika nyumba za watu;   alikaa
Here formerly   cat   did-not-stay   place   houses of men;   he-stayed

mwituni   au   maguguni tu.   Paka mmoja alikuwa rafiki ya sungura
in-forest   or   in-bush   only.   Cat   1   he-was friend of   hare

wakatembea   pamoja,   na   paka   akastaajabia   werevu   wa
and-they-wandered   together   and   cat   and-he-admired   cleverness   of

rafiki   yake;   lakini siku moja   funo   akagombana   na
friend   his   but   day   1   duiker   and-he-argued-together   with

sungura   akamwua   kwa pembe zake.   Sasa kwa kuwa   rafiki
hare   and-he-him-killed   with   horns his.   then   of   to-be   friend

yake   amekufa   paka   akafuatana   na   yule   funo.
his   he-is-dead   cat   and-he-accompanied   with   this (the)   duiker.

> A long time ago the cat did not live in men's houses: he lived only in the forest or in the bush. A certain cat was the friend of a hare and wandered about with him; the cat admired the cleverness of his friend, but, one day, a duiker quarreled with the hare and killed him with a thrust of his horns. Since his friend was dead, the cat began keeping company with the duiker.

Whatever its status is in the classification of African languages (family? subfamily? branch?), the Bantu group remains the most important one from a demographic viewpoint, having some 60 million speakers; linguistically it is the most homogeneous. It is precisely to demonstrate the extent and limit of this homogeneity that I shall present a second example, borrowed from a language geographically and linguistically as far away from Swahili as possible. This is Bulu, a language of the Southern Cameroon, which authors such as Miss Homburger have refused to consider as Bantu. Hers is a minority opinion, contradicted as effectively by the classic works of Meinhof as by the recent works of Guthrie.

In order to facilitate comparison, instead of giving a text recorded in the field, I have myself translated the Swahili example presented above. It will not be elegant Bulu, then; mine is barely correct, but it is comprehensible to a well-disposed Bulu. I shall give only one sentence in the standard transcription called "American" (although it is the work of an Englishman) or "Protestant," used by the American Presbyterian Mission. The two main defects of this transcription are that it does not note tones and (even more than in the standard transcription of Swahili) it separates into several parts segments which really constitute single entities:

Mam me kuba a nga bo na, ésingi é nji ke tabe e nda ya bôt, ve tabe afan a bilok étam étam.

The following is the phonological transcription with an interlinear translation (the low tones are noted only on the consonants, except for one exception intended to underline the contrast):

ḿam   mɛ́-kubá   áŋgábɔɔ   náà, esíŋi énjíkɛtɔɔ́   ɛ́-ndá
things of the past it there happened that cat did-not-stay in-house(s)

yǎ bot, vɛ̆tabɛ   áfan   á-bilɔ́ʔ etám-etám. Esíŋi eziŋ émbɛ́
of men and-stayed in-forest and-grass only-only. Cat a-certain was

ŋgbʷɛ́ngbʷaa ókpʷeŋ ńdɛ-hŋ́ béŋgábɔɔ   béwuluʔu   ǹsámbá
friend   of-"hare" thus-and they-did they-walked-always company

wúá, ńdɛ-hŋ́ esíŋi éséme   feʔ ebélɛ wé; ńdɛ-hŋ́ móɂ̀
1   thus-and cat he-admires wisdom friend his; thus-and day

eziŋ   zib bá ókpʷeŋ vɛ̆lúman   á   zib èwóe ókpʷeŋ
a-certain duiker they "hare" and-fought and duiker kills "hare"

ńlak. Amú   náa, móé ẁé awúyâ esíŋi éŋgàtoŋ
with-horn. Reason that friend his he-is-dead cat begins-to-follow

zib ètɛ̆.
duiker this.

Even in such a short text, the higher proportion of monosyllables and the frequency of closed syllables (i.e., syllables ending in a consonant) is immediately noticeable. It can be demonstrated that the final etymological vowel of CB has been replaced by an "invisible vowel" (unstable suffix) whose tone has passed onto the preceding syllable. There are few similarities of vocabulary in the two examples.

2.   NON-BANTU CLASS LANGUAGES:
WEST ATLANTIC GROUP

FULANI

The language of the Fulani, of which various dialects are spoken from the Atlantic to the Nile by communities with different numerical importance living in Sudanic and Sahelian zones, belongs typologically to the languages called "class languages." The characteristic structures of these languages have been particularly well preserved in the Fulani group: not only do we find genders, each of which is characterized by a pair of primary classifiers in the plurality:nonplurality opposition, but we also find that all the nominals (with a few rare exceptions) are formed by adding a "class suffix" to a root or to a theme coming from this root. These suffixes are phonematically reminiscent of a classifier's composition, and they may vary between several "degrees," depending on the nominal involved. We find, thus, among the nominals under the jurisdiction of the "gender" ~*gol-di*, the following forms of the singular:

kof~*gol*, "greeting" [4th-degree suffix: C (nasalized stop)-V-(C′)]
boggol, "rope" [3rd-degree suffix C (stop)--V-(C′)]
derewol, "paper" [2nd-degree suffix C (continued)-V-(C′)]
kurol, "arrow" [1st-degree suffix: -V(C′)][7]

The relationships which exist between a nominal and its determinants are marked by the suffixation to the determinant of a degree—variable according to the determinant involved—of the classifier of the nominal. Obviously, we are in the presence of an extremely constraining and redundant system, but the use of this system, sometimes rather delicate, allows for extreme precision in the expression of a thought. Let me point out that Fulani also involves a verbal system which is formally differentiated, rather complex, and characterized by a group of markers suffixed to the verbal radical (or to its extensions), but which does not involve a tonal system.

7. Note that certain classifiers do not have the fourth degree of suffixation indicated above. Such is the case for those with an initial consonant which cannot be nasalized in the Fulani phonology (/k/, /b/, or /d/, for example) and which because of this have no fourth degree. For other reasons, presumably to avoid confusion, classifiers with an initial / ~d/ have no first degree and use instead the second degree. Finally, suffixes for the classifier *be* are always phonetically identical with this classifier.

The following text was collected from a young man from Garoua (North Cameroon), who was, at the time, ten years old. It is quite characteristic of the Fulani spoken by the urbanized people in central Adamawa, a Fulani characterized by a certain number of spreading traits.

> *gorgiraaɓe   tato/ ~buubu kurori bee   leebol   ɓe*
> Age companions   three "Fly" "Flour" and "Fresh Butter" They

~bii ɓe ~defa niiri / ~buubu wii   naman   ~gawri / hoosi ~gawri
said they cook porridge "Fly"   say will smash millet   took millet

mum dilli hayre /   leebol   dilli jamnugo   yiite /   kurori dilli
his left stone   "Fresh Butter" left to light   fire   "Flour" left

ⁱooɓugo ~diyam/ ~buubu goo ʾo   don   nama   wadi
to draw water   "Fly" him   he is-in-midst to crush make action

di ~bo /   ~der   di~boto   ~go   di~bande   ʾoon   goo
of shaking   in   repeated shaking this trepidation that   she

doʾini   dum/ hoore mum tuggi dow hayre/ daa~de yewi waati/
made to fall him head his carried on stone neck broke split

kurori   hoosi tummude ~gappere/ pedi ~diyam   don warta /
"Flour" took calabash   hole   drew water is-in-midst-return

nii ʾo joʾini ~de haa dow hoore mum gam   ~gappere/ sey
thus he placed   it   on   head that because hold   only

~diyam   joofi   ʾilni dum/ nonnon soobaajo mabbe tatabo goo/
water   leaked carried him thus   friend   their third   he

nani   soobaaʾen   pat   maaydi /   doggi   do
understood friends   all   are dead together ran   there

don warta   bee yulbere/ nii ´yulbere   wulidi   mo/ /daa
is-in-midst-return with cinders thus cinders   burn entirely him so

soobiraaɓe tato fuu maayi /.
friends   three all are dead.

Three age companions—"Fly," "Flour," and "Fresh Butter"—said that they were preparing some porridge. "Fly" said that he would pound the millet; he took his millet and left for the millstone. "Fresh Butter" left to light the fire, "Flour" went to draw some water. "Fly," while pounding [the millet], made [the earth] shake. This repeated shaking [brought about] a vibration which made him fall down; his head touching on the millstone, his neck breaking, he died. "Flour" took a perforated calabash, drew some water, and returned. Because of the perforations, he put the calabash on his head, but the water ran out and carried him away. When their third companion understood that all of his friends had died, he ran out with a firebrand, so that the firebrand consumed him entirely. Thus did the three all die.

3.   LANGUAGES WITHOUT CLASSES:
HAMITO-SEMITIC FAMILY (?)

HAUSA

Hausa (Hausanci), with probably twelve million speakers, is the second language of Black Africa, after Swahili. They have in common a large percentage of vocabulary of Arabic origin, but there the resemblance ends. In the first place, on the sociological level, we should note that the Hausawa are much more numerous than the Waswahili: there are five to seven million Hausawa, of whom two-thirds live in Northern Nigeria and the rest in eastern Niger; and there is a significant diaspora in all of West Africa, even as far as the Congo, the Mediterranean (Tripoli in Libya), and the Red Sea (Suakim and Djeddah). The diffusion of Hausa beyond tribal limits results from economic and historical phenomena which resemble those which favored the diffusion of Swahili or of Mande-Dyula. In the first place, the Hausa have a long commercial tradition: from the "urban ports" of the southern Saharan Sahel, Gobir, Sokoto, and Kano, they guaranteed the distribution of merchandise coming by caravans from the Mediterranean Basin to the forest zone and returning with cola nuts, ivory, and slaves. In the second place, after the Fulani Uthman dan Fodio had united the Hausa city-states into a powerful empire after his holy war at the beginning of the nineteenth century, it was their language which became the official language of this empire and which spread with it almost to the present borders of the Northern Region of Nigeria. The British, finally, maintained and consolidated this privileged position, so that, at independence, Hausa was chosen as the official language of the Northern Region, with seventeen million inhabitants,[8] and it was even mentioned as a possible common federal language for all of Nigeria.

Hausa was written down very early, probably from the fourteenth century and perhaps even before, in Arabic characters, and it possesses a fairly extensive literature, which has been only partially classified. It is used in primary education, on the radio, in the press, and in the administration. All of the legislation inherited from the colonial period is now being translated, even the rules of cricket and polo.

8. This idea did not fail to arouse local reactions, which degenerated into bloody riots, at least among the Tiv of the Lower Benue (1960 to 1964).

Here we have to do, then, with one of the best-known languages of Africa, yet linguists are far from being in agreement on its genetic relationships. Delafosse considered it to be Negro-African; Greenberg classifies it as "Afro-Asiatic" or, in the terminology of the French school, Hamito-Semitic—related, then, to Berber and Arabic and to those languages called "Cushitic" (Ethiopia and Somali); Westermann and the British school speak, with some difficulty, of "Chado-Hamitic," which seems to imply an intermediary position that, in the final analysis, may not be without merit.

The Hamito-Semitic relationship was proposed in the middle of the past century and is based on morphological traits such as the following:

(1) the existence of a masculine and a feminine, the latter marked by a /t/, as in Arabic or Berber.

(2) the use of a morpheme of annexion /n/, as in classical Egyptian or in Berber.

(3) the resemblances between pronominal systems, especially certain possessives in /k/ and certain subject pronouns.

(4) the common existence of a prefix /m/ to form nouns of agent and nouns of place.

To this argument, the partisans of the Negro-African link (Niger-Kordofanian, in Greenberg) reply with examples of the following traits:

(1) the existence of suffixes such as /wa/ and /ci/, which recall in a striking way the Bantu prefixes /*ba/ and /*ki/: *hausawa,* "the Hausa"; *waswahili,* "the Swahili"; *Hausanci,* "the Hausa language"; *Kiswahili,* "the Swahili language; *ciLuba,* "the Luba language." The prefix /m/, noted above, can also be interpreted as an argument in favor of the Negro-African linkage.

(2) the existence of a system of tones, which, up to a certain point, allows for the establishment of morphological classes.

(3) the form of certain of the autonomous pronouns, an argument which is as ambiguous as that concerning the prefix /m/.

(4) the existence of an actualizer or a copula (equivalent of "to be"), *nee,* recalling CB *ni.

Arguments based on the vocabulary are equally ambiguous: as partisans of one or the other theory, linguists consider as borrowings either those elements linked to Hamito-Semitic or those linked to Negro-African.

I have myself come to the point where I wonder if we are not in the presence of a pidgin which became successful, that is, a very antique trade language which evolved while preserving and developing, through constant interference, characteristics borrowed from one or another of the linguistic groups initially in contact with it. The theory of mixed languages, of *Mischsprache*, is highly discredited today, since many people have abused it. Perhaps this theory might be the one to best explain the realities of Hausa. I dare not be too affirmative on this point, although I do know that some Soviet linguists have occupied themselves with similar questions, even if they have not reached similar conclusions.

In any case, we can list in a very brief and general way the following characteristics of the Hausa language:

(a) five vowels; three implosive consonants /ɓ, ɗ, 'y/, two ejectives /ƙ, ts/, one retroflex flapped /ʀ/ in opposition to a trilled /r/.

(b) significant vocalic lengths.

(c) a system of tones with two levels.

(d) all syllables begin with a consonant, although the standard orthography does not mark the initial glottal occlusive /ʔ/.

(e) a complex system of prefixes and suffixes as verbal and nominal formatives.

(f) formation of plural nouns obeying complicated rules, among others reduplication and suffixation.

(g) opposition of a masculine and a feminine marked only in the singular for nominals and pre-verbs. The gender is not recognizable by the shape of the independent nominal only but rather by the agreements which it governs.

(h) formation of verbs derived by suffixation and, sometimes, by mutation of the vowels of the radical.

(i) conjugation operates with the help of pre-verbs, or pronoun subjects, indicating both person, gender, and number as well as the verbal aspect or tense.

The text to provide an example was furnished to me by my colleague, Claude Gouffé, professor of Hausa at the Ecole des Langues Orientales.

HAUSA TEXT

1. *Standard Orthography Used in Nigeria*

[Usefulness of Agricultural Expositions]

Nunin Amfanin Gona a Jihar Arewa, muhimmin abu ne ƙwarai da gaske, ba ma domin saboda ɗan kyautar da manoma su ke samu ba ne kawai, aʔa, har ma ta ƙara waye wa manoma kai da kuma ƙarfafa musu zuciya don su yi noma mai kyau yadda za su sami amfani mafi daraja tare da yalwa. Kamar yadda aka saba nune-nunen amfanin gona a larduna na

Jihar Arewa da zaran manoma sun kawad da amfaninsu, a bana ma haka a ke ta faman yi a ko ina cikin Jihar Arewa. Ana yin wadannan kuwa ba domin kome ba ne sai don a ƙara taimakon manoma da masu sanaʔa wajen wayad da su don su bi kyakkyawar hanya ta inganta sanaʔoʔinsu. (Extract from *Gaskiya Ta Fi Kwabo*, no. 1.145, 17 January 1964, p. 16, columns 3–5.)

2. *Phonological Transcription*

N.B.—In this transcription the capital letters of the standard orthography have been omitted because they have no linguistic meaning. However, the punctuation of the standard orthography has been retained. Also, within the framework of each of the three sentences (numbered I, II, III) of which the Hausa text is composed, the numbers placed under each "word" refer to the corresponding English referent in the literal translation.

I. *nuunìn ʔàmfàanin goonaa ʔà jihàr ʔaRèewa, mùhimmìn ʔàbù nee*
   1   2   3   4 5   6   7   8 9

kʷarai dà gàske, bàa maa dòomin sabòo dà dan kʸàutar dà manòomaa su
 10   11   12   13 14   15   16 17 18   19   20   21   22

kèe saamùu ba nèe kawài, ʔaaʔàa, har maa ta ƙaaRà waayèe wà manòomaa
 23   24   25 26   27   28   29 30 31 32   33 34   35

kai dà kumaa ƙaRfàfaa musù zuucìyaa don sù yi noomaa mài kʸaù yaddà
 36 37   38   39   40   41   42 43 44   45   46 47   48

zaa sù sàami ʔàmfàanii mafìi darajàa tàaRe dà yàlwaa.
 49 50 51   52   53   54   55 56   57

II. *kàmar yaddà ʔakà saabà nùune-nùunen ʔàmfàanin goonaa ʔà*
   1   2   3   4   5   6   7   8

lardunàa na jihàr ʔaRèewa dà zaaRan manòomaa sun kawad dà ʔàmfàanin
 9   10 11   12   13   14   15   16   17 18   19

sù, ʔà bana maa hakà ʔa kèe ta faaman yiì ʔà koo ʔìnaa cikin jihàr
 20 21   22   23   24 25 26 27   28   29 30 31   32   33   34

ʔaRèewa.
  35

III. *ʔa nàa yiǹ wadànnan kùwaa bàa dòomin koomee ba nèe sai don*
    1 2 3   4   5   6   7   8   9 10 11 12

ʔà ƙaaRà tàimakon manòomaa dà màasu sànaʔàa wajen waayad dà suu
 13 14   15   16   17   18   19   20   21 22 23

don sù bi kʸàkkʸaawar hanyàa ta ʔingàntà sanaʔooʔin sù.
 24 25 26   27   28   29   30   31   32

3. *Literal Translation*

I. exposition-of / harvest-of / field / in / region-of / north, / importance
      1   2   3   4   5   6   7

of / thing / it is / completely / with / truth, / not / certainly / for /
   8   9   10   11   12   13   14   15

because / of / son-of / gift-of / that / farmers / they / have the habit to /
   16   17   18   19   20   21   22   23

obtain / (not) / it is / only, / not, / until / certainly / by the fact that /
   24   25   26   27   28   29   30   31

to augment / to enlighten / to / farmers / head / and / also / reinforce /
     32   33   34   35   36   37   38   39

to them / heart / for that / they / make / crops / that which has / excel-
   40   41   42   43   44   45   46   47

lence / so that / go / they / to obtain / harvest / superior [in] /
   48   49   50   51   52   53

quality / together / with / abundance.
   54   55   56   57

   II. resemblance-of / way that / one has / taken the habit [to] /
           1   2   3   4

show-here-and-there / harvest-of / field / in / provinces / those-of / region-
           5   6   7   8   9   10   11

of / north / with / simultaneity-of / farmers / they have / made to change
12   13   14   14   15   16   17

the place / for / harvest-of / theirs / in / this-here year / certainly / in that
   18   19   20   21   22   22   23   24

way / one / is in the midst of / applying himself to / war-of / to make /
  25   26   27   27   28   29

in / no matter / where / in / region-of / north.
30   31   32   33   34   35

   III. one / is in the midst of / to make-of / these [things] there / also /
          1   2   3   4   5

not / for / whatever may be / (not) / it is / only / in order that / one /
  6   7   8   9   10   11   12   13

increases / help-of / farmers / and / those who have / profession / on the
    14   15   16   17   18   19   20

side-of / to make understand / to / them / in order that / they / follow /
   21   22   23   24   25   26

good [in fact] of / way / that of / reinforcing / professions-of / them.
      27   28   29   30   31   32

4. *Free Translation*

In the Northern Region the agricultural exposition is an extremely important event, not so much because of the small prizes that the farmers receive there, certainly, but rather because it offers an opportunity for the farmers to learn about developments and because of the way in which it encourages them to work their lands with better techniques, in order that they may obtain a harvest which is superior in both quality and quantity. In accordance with the practice which has been set up to increase the number of agricultural expositions in the provinces of the Northern Region as soon as the farmers have harvested their crops, this year again we are trying to organize them everywhere in the Northern Region. Obviously, these organizations have no other end in view than to help the farmers and the professional people by bringing them lights which will enable them to follow the best path for developing their profession.

4. CLASSLESS LANGUAGES: NILO-SAHARAN FAMILY

SONGHAÏ

Songhaï (Sŏray in Timbuktu, Soŋay in Gao) is spoken by a total of about 700,000 speakers living in an area ranging along the Niger River from north of Mopti up to the Nigerian frontier; its widest territorial extension lies within the eastern part of its domain (*cercles* of Tillabery, Tera, Niamey, and Dosso). It includes several dialects which can be generally divided into two groups, a western one extending to about 30 kilometers east of Timbuktu, and an eastern one including the dialect of the Niger Valley up to the Mali-Niger frontier, that of the Kaado country (Tillabery-Tera), the Wogo of the Niger Valley around Zinder, the Jerma (northeast of Tillabery, Niamey, and Dosso), the Dendi (Gaya, Parakou, and Kandi in Dahomey). The following text belongs to the dialect of Timbuktu and was collected from Ibrahim Mahaman, about twenty-three years of age. Spoken by a community with a long urban tradition, strongly penetrated by foreign influences, particularly by Arabic ones, this language is characterized, on the morphosyntactic level, by less complete structures than those of the eastern dialects and, on the lexical level, by a large number of loanwords, coming particularly from the Arabic and secondarily from Bambara.

hõ   ci jingarey   ber   jingarey   goy / a   hima   boro kur ma-yahadar
today   is mosque   large   mosque   work   it   is good   man   all   be present

mise   wo kuna / hõ   a   hima   yirkɔy   baŋa diyo   kur   ma-goy
event   this   in   today   it is good   God   slave   the   all   that they work

~guyo   hiney   hinne yirkɔy   hu   wo kuna / wodi ci haya kaana
their   possibility   level   God   house   this   in   this   is thing   that

boro   kur   go-hima   ka-dam   ~gu   suba-kanido   se / ka-jooga   ja
man   all   is good   to-do   his   tomorrow-rest   for   to take   since

Padduha   har   jaari-maasu   boro go-goy   ~da   Panniya   ~da   bine
morning   until   day-middle   man   work   with   goodwill   with   heart

feerey | boro diibi laabu wala boro go-lenje   ꝑalhor   boro go-sãnfa
open   man molds clay   or   man carries chalky stone man   sands
wala boro go-yar | wey   diyo binde baa   di   ci ma | hari
or   man polishes woman them then leaves there is what? water
gur   don   ～da kobi   ～da tubal   kar   ～da
to draw to sing with clapping of hands and   drum hitting and
kolo   kar   ～da ka-hina har diyo ŋaa di | ꝑalaasara ci
small drum to beat and to cook male they food the   evening is
ꝑalfatina   ꝑalwakati bɔrɔ kur goy ka-ben   saa   di | i
Profession of Faith   time   man all work finish moment the he
kar   batu   ka-wir   yirkɔy kuna hinje ～da   tuubi |.
form assembly   to ask   God   in   Pardon and Benediction.

Today the neighborhood of the Great Mosque is working to [repair] the mosque. It is proper for all men to participate in this event and that all the slaves of God work on this House according to their capabilities. This is an excellent thing for each man to do in view of his fate in the beyond. Each works from morning to midday with a resolute and joyous heart! One molds the clay, another carries the stone, another sands it, and another smooths it (the plaster). What, then, is the role of the women? They draw water, clap their hands, play on the large and small drums, and prepare food for the men. In the evening the moment of the Prayer arrives and the end of work; the men meet together and ask God's pardon and blessing.

5. LANGUAGES WITHOUT CLASSES: MANDE GROUP

The Mande group is probably the most important in the Western Sudan, with about twenty million speakers (in Senegal, Mali, Guinea, Portuguese Guinea, Gambia, Upper Volta, Ghana, Sierra Leone, Liberia, Niger, and Mauritania). For a long time a distinction has been made between a southern subgroup and a northern subgroup, called "Mande-Tan" and "Mande-Fu" on the basis of the two roots of the word "ten"; but this division has recently been questioned.

Tones play a more important role in the languages of the south than in the languages of the north, where their existence was not perceived by European authors for a long time.

There is a high frequency of *disyllabic roots* of the kind CVCV, CVN, or CVV. The monosyllabic roots seem often to be the result of the reduction of disyllabic roots.

Compounding is a frequent process for the formation of words, for verbs as well as nouns:

da-bo: mouth–to take away = to wean; *da-ja*: mouth–to dry = to be tired.

da-ji: mouth–water = saliva; *nyɛ-ji*: eye–water = tear (Mandinka).

There is also a well-developed system of suffixal derivation, suffixes being functional morphemes expressing notions such as agent, abstention, manner, etc., or grammatical categories: the verb and its aspects, number, etc.

Example from Mande-Tan: Mandinka (Malinke) of Kankan:

bi	*káro-nyi*	*telé*	*tã*	*ni senyi,*	*ŋ-ye-kúmala*	*nyɛ*	*ŋ-fá*
today	month-this	day	10	and 8	I speak	you	my-father

kã	*dɔ, mɛ̃*	*ye*	*manĩkamɔri-kǎ*	*ŋ-na*	*kúmafɔlɔ*	*ye*	*mɛ̃*
language	in, this	to-be	Malinke-language	my	first-word	to-be	that

di,	*wole*	*ye*	*ŋ- báda*	*bálɔkɔ*	*di,*
(actualizer)	this	to-be	my-domicile	question-of-food	(actualizer),

baáwa bálo	*ye*	*gbɛlɛyala*	*samále*	*dɔ jamaná kɔ́nɔ.*
reason food	to-be	made-difficult	rainy-season	in country in.

Today, the eighteenth of the month, I am speaking to you in the language of my father, which is Malinke. My first word concerns the question of food among us, for food is difficult to find in this land during the rainy season.

káro-nyi: noun + *nyi*: noun + particle of determination. Notice the order of the words: "month-this day 18" = "18th day of the month." In the same way:

ŋ-fá: "me-father" = "father of me"; the *nomen regens* follows the *nomen rectum*.

ŋ: pronominal particle, 1st person singular.

ye: particle of actualization "to be," used in composition as a functional morpheme of the present.

kúmala: *kúma*, "word," *-la*, verbal postposition; *ŋ-ye-kúma-la*, "me to be-word-verbal marker."

ye . . . di: discontinuous actualizer.

mɛ̃: neutral demonstrative pronoun with a relative value.

ŋ-na: "of me, to me."

wole: emphatic demonstrative.

bálɔkɔ: *bálɔ*, "nourishment," *kɔ* "question," with vowel harmony.

gbélɛyala; *gbélɛ*, "difficulty"; *ya*: causative morpheme; *la*: verbal postposition.

samále: *samá*, "rainy season" + emphatic particle *le* (cf. *wole*).

Example from Mande-Fu: Susu of Lower Guinea:

ŋ ma bằxí   tĭ   fɔlɔmà   tìná.   kúyé íbà,   wǒ sìgámà   ŋ
I of house to make   will begin tomorrow.   Day clears, we will leave I
ma bằxí rákèlidè. ŋ   bárà   bɛ̆dɛ́   gé,   wúrí bárà   sɛ̀gɛ́.
of house to raise.   I [completed] earth to dig, wood dug has-been.

ségétéla   wúyáxì   fámà   bɛ̆dɛ́ máxanìdè.   yɛ̀xɛ̂ kérɛ̆nắ
Young-people numerous will come earth to carry off. Lamb it is
bámà   e   xɔ̆tɔ́yì   ra.
will-be-set-apart them meal for.

> The construction of my house will begin tommorow. At daybreak we
> will leave to erect my house. I have dug the earth, the wood has been cut.
> Many young people will come to take the earth away. It is a lamb which
> will be offered for their meal.

ŋ ma bằxí: 1st person pronoun + connecting particle + *nomen regens*:
"I-of-house" = "my house."

fɔlɔmà: *fɔlɔ*, "to begin"; *-mà*: morpheme of a projective aspect; cf.
sìgámá, fámà, bámà.

rákèlidè: *kèli*, "to raise"; *rá-*, morpheme of intention; *-dè*, gerundive
suffix; cf. *má-xánì-dè.*

bárà . . . gé: vb. *gé*, "to dig," preceded by the morpheme *bárà*, inchoative
completed; cf. *bára sègé*, where *sègé* is the simple radical.

kérɛ̆nắ: *kèrɛ̆*, "1" + emphatic particle *-nã.*

e: third person plural pronoun.

ra: "for," particle of intention, same root as *rá-* in *rákèlidè.*

6. LANGUAGES WITHOUT CLASSES: KWA GROUP

This group spreads along the coast from the mouth of the Niger to
the Liberia–Ivory Coast frontier and includes about twenty million
speakers (in Nigeria, Dahomey, Togo, Ghana, and Ivory Coast).

The phonology and tonology of these languages are complex. The
tones play a role which is given more importance by the fact that the
roots of words are monosyllabic and that many homophonic series are
distinguished only by tone.[9] There is no morphological distinction
between verbal and nominal roots. Morphology is very slight: "words"
are formed by composition rather than by derivation; the grammar and

9. The phonological transcription of Yoruba used here postulates three tones:
high (´), low (`), and middle (not marked).

syntax are a bit reminiscent of those in Chinese. There is no grammatical gender, but there are traces of nominal classes in several languages of Ghana (Twi) and Togo (Avatimɛ, Akpɔso).

An example from Yoruba: Yoruba has more than five million speakers; the main language of the Kwa group, it is spoken in Western Nigeria, Dahomey, and Togo. The transcription established a century ago by the Anglican archbishop, Crowther, a descendant of slaves of Yoruba origin and one of the great figures in African history, is still old-fashioned, despite some reforms of details. It is unlikely that the transcription will ever be totally revised, given the importance of literature written with the traditional orthography; the example given below is thus taken from a recent novel by D. O. Fagungwa, *Igbo Olodumare* ("The Bush of God") (Edinburgh: Nelson, 1960), page 34.

Wo mi, ọrẹ, mi, gbe o ju soke, o ju ni ọrọ wa, Ọlọrun tobi l'Ọba, ma ṣọra, ma ṣọra, ma ṣọra ki o to ma ṣata ọmọnikeji rẹ, nitori baba mi ni o ma nkede fun gbogbo araye wipe ki nwọn ki o maṣe dẹṣẹ mọ, iyalẹnu lo si jẹ lọjọ na, nigbati on papa ri i wipe iwa ti on wipe ki awọn enia o maṣe hu wọnni ni on papa nhu, ẹṣẹ ti on wipe ki awọn ọmọ araiye maṣe da ni on na papa nda, irin ti on wipe ki enia maṣe rin ri on papa nrin, ọrọ ti on wipe ki awọn ọmọ araiye maṣe ṣọ ni on papa nṣọ, itiju pade itiju, ni ọjọ ti baba mi ri ẹṣẹ wọnni ninu iwe onibode, nibiti onitọhun to wọn si gadagba gadagba.[10]

Look at me, friend, look at me: we must look each other in the face in order to discuss. God is great in his power. Be careful, be very careful, before accusing your neighbor of something. My father was in the habit of urging people not to sin; he was astounded on the day that he realized that the very acts which he condemned he had himself personally committed. The sins that he had asked others not to commit, he had committed them himself; the paths from which he had discouraged them, he had taken them himself; the words which he had forbidden them to use, he had himself pronounced. Shame met shame face to face the day that my father saw his sins clearly written on the book of the Keeper of the Gates.

Phonological Transcription

wò	mì	ɔréɛ̀mi,	gbé ojú s(í)	òkè;	ojú ni	ɔ̀rɔ́
look at	me	friend of me,	lift eye to go	up-high;	eye it is	discussion
				= hill	subordination by	

wà.	ɔlɔ́rũ	tóbi	lɔ́ba.	máa	šɔ́ra,	máa	šɔ́ra,
comes.	God	is-great	in kingdom.	Watch over	body	watch over	body

anteposition   *ní ɔba > lɔ́ba*   aspective of the continuous   *šɔ́ra < šɔ́ ara*

10. *ṣ = š; ọ = ɔ; ẹ = ɛ.*

máa	*šɔ́ra,*	*k(í)o tó*	*šáátà*	*ɔmɔnĭkejĭirɛ*
watch over	body,	before	to-say-any-evil	about your neighbor
		= that you arrive		*ɔmɔ* = child, *ɛni* = person,
				ĭkejĭ = second, *rɛ* = your

nítoríi	*bàbáami*	*ló*	*máa ń kêde*		*fũ*	*gbogbo*
because	my father	it is he	cried-outside		so that	all
ní = in,		*ló < ni ó*	*kêde < ke* = cry,			
ĭti = origin,			*òde* = outside			
cause,						
orí = head,						
i = genitive						
particle						

aráyé	*wí*	*kpé*	*kí*	*wɔ̃*	*má še*	*déšὲ*
human-types	to say	to declare	that	they	not-to do	to sin
ara = inhabitant,					*dà* = create,	
ayé = world					*èšὲ* = sin	

mɔ̃.	*ìyà*	*lénu*	*ló*	*si*	*jέ*	*lɔ́jɔ́ nɔ́ɔ*	*nígbà tí òũ*
still.	opening	in-mouth	it is	[connective]	was	this-day-then	when he
verbid,			*ló < ní ó*			*lɔ́jɔ́ < ní ɔjɔ́*	*nígbà < ní igbà*
"to continue"							

pàápàá	*rí-i*	*wí kpé ìwà*	*tí*	*òũ*	*wí*	*kpé*	*àwɔ̃ èniyɔ̀*
himself	saw-that	that trait	that	him	to say	to declare	them persons
		"to say" +					
		"to declare"					

ó má še	*hù*	*wɔ̃ɔ̃*	*nì*	*lòũ*	*pàápàá*	*ń hù*
he not to do	behave	them	that	it-is-that-he	himself	behaved
		wɔ̃ = plurative		*lòũ < ni òũ*		*ń* = contin-
		partitive, *òũ* =				uous aspect
		he, the				

èšὲ	*tì*	*òũ wí*	*kpé*	*kí*	*àwɔ̃ ɔmaaráyé*		*má še*	*dá*
sin	that	he said	to declare	that	they humans		not to do	to create
					ɔma = child,			
					ará = inhabitant,			
					ayé = world			

lòũ	*pàápàá*	*ń dá;*	*ĭrĩ̀*	*tí*	*òũ wí*	*kpé*	*kì*	*èniyɔ̀*
it-is-he	self	he-created;	to ask	that	he said	to declare	that	no-one
lòũ < ni òũ								

má še rĩ̀	*lòũ*	*pàápàá*	*ń rĩ̀;*	*ɔrɔ̀*	*tí*	*òũ wí kpé kí àwɔ̃ ɔmaaráyé*
not-do	it is-he	self	he-do;	thing	that	he-say that they humans

má še sɔ	*lòũ*	*pàápàá*	*ń sɔ.*	*ìtìjú*	*kpàdé*	*ìtìjú*	*lɔ́jɔ́*	*tí*
not-to-say	it is-he	self	he say.	shame	meets	shame	it is-day	that
				i = nominal			*lɔ́jɔ́ < ní ɔjɔ́*	
				prefix; *tì* =				
				to close;				
				ojú = eye				

bàbáàmí   ri   ɛ̌šɛ̀ wɔ̌ɔ n nínú   *ìwé   oníbodè*
father-of-me sees sin these in   book keeper-of-door
                    ní = in,   *o* = prefix of agent,
                    inú = chest   *ní* = to possess,
                                            bodè = gate of city
  níbi   tí   onítɔ̀hṹ   *tò   wɔ́   sí gàdàgbà-gadagba.*
  in-place that this latter   arranges them in   clearly.
  níbi < ní ìbi   *o + ní + tí,*
                    "of" + *ɔhṹ,* "there"

7. TRADE LANGUAGES: PIDGINS AND CREOLES

Contact with Europeans, particularly since the colonial partition, has involved the appearance or the development of Euro-African lingua francas, whose vocabulary is largely European (especially English and Portuguese), while the grammar and syntax are African and generally derive from the vernacular languages spoken in the regions where these pidgins or Creoles have developed.

For sociological and political reasons, there has been almost no development of a pigdin of this type based on French. This is largely due to the fact that French was the only language officially used in administration and education. "Petit-Nègre" is widespread only in cheap adventure novels and comic strips: even its name is rarely used in West Africa, where one speaks rather of "Français-tirailleur" or "Français-tiraillou" to designate the deformed French used in the army or on construction sites by Africans who did not have the chance to go to school. It is a language without prestige, regarded as comic by educated Africans, used in contemporary African literature in a way reminiscent of the pseudo-patois of Molière's peasants or of Nucingen's accent in Balzac. Until now, it has always remained at the level of an auxiliary jargon, to which its users themselves prefer either French or an African language.

On the other hand, pidgins and Creoles with an English or Portuguese lexical base have given birth or are now giving birth to real languages: Krio in Sierra Leone is already such a real language; Kriyol in Portuguese Guinea and the Cape Verde Islands is another; the Pidgin or Coast English of Western Cameroon was close to becoming one,[11] but

11. Kitchen Kaffir or Isipiki or Fanekalo of southern Africa is now being rejected by the Africans in this region, who look at it, quite correctly, as a form of discrimination deliberately perpetrated by the Whites, who virtually refuse them the right to speak standard English or Afrikaans.

independence may result in a setback, to the profit of standard English or French. Here are some examples of two of these idioms:

(A)   KRIYOL OR PURTUGUES IN SENEGAMBIA

Spoken in Portuguese Guinea, in the Cape Verde Islands, in the Senegalese Casamance, in Gambia, and on the "Little Coast" of Senegal as far as Dakar. In Senegal it is spoken as a first language by more than 50,000 people; as a lingua franca it is spoken by at least twice this number. It is in retreat, particularly in the face of French. The vocabulary is predominantly Portuguese. The morphosyntax shows strong West Atlantic (Wolof, Serer) and Mande (Mandinka) influences. The phonology of standard Portuguese has, in the same way, been modified by interference from the African linguistic milieu.[12]

Lifãti	*ki-ũguli*	*kúku*	*i-fiẽsa*	*na*	*si*
Elephant	who-swallow	coconut	he-has-confidence	with	his

kadéra.	*Kela*	*sédi*	*ka-bu-kumesa*	*kúsa*	*ku*	*bu-sebo*	*kuma*
behind.	That	means	not-begin	thing	that	you-know	like

ka-ta-kabãta-l.
will-not-achieve.

> If an elephant swallows a coconut, it mean he trusts his behind, which means that one should never begin what one does not know how to bring to a good end.

(B)   PIDGIN OR KOS INGILIS OF CAMEROON

Spoken in the Cameroon, at Douala, along the railroad up to Nkong-samba, in the Bamileke Massif all along the old French-English frontier (now a provincial limit), and in eastern Nigeria, the length of the Cameroonian frontier and the Cross River down to the sea; important enclaves in all Cameroonian cities. Perhaps a million speakers? It forms a kind of dialect of a lingua franca which is spoken all along the Atlantic Coast from Bathurst to Bata. Its vocabulary is predominantly English (although it has retained in many cases words which are almost identical in French and in English), with some Portuguese, Spanish, and African (Yoruba, Hausa, Ewe, and northwest Bantu) elements. The morphosyntax has an African aspect, but with particular traits which belong to no language in the region (a region characterized, it

12. See A. Chataigner, "Le 'Créole Portugais' du Sénégal," *Journal of African Languages*, II, pt. 1 (1963).

must be emphasized, by extreme linguistic heterogeneity). The phonology, absolutely paradoxical, sometimes seems to defy all recognized rules and deserves a special study by itself. Currently the language is expanding, but it might diminish in the face of the development of French and English in primary education.[13]

> *Soja   don-giv   tiit   foo ndundu dis taym.*
> Soldier have-given teeth for vagina this time.
> "The army has made the price of certain services rise sharply."

soja: "soldier"; *tiit*: "teeth"; *dis*: "this"; *taym*: "time."

don-giv: "to give," with *don-* (from "done"), aspective of the completed.

foo: "for," locative particle and general instrumental, calqued on northwest Bantu; notice that [*foo*] is the normal phonological reconstruction for both French /*pur*/ "pour" and English "for."

ndundu: "vagina," Bantu word, probably Malimba—the only African word in the sentence.

dis taym: exact calque, or literal translation, of several African expressions which are equivalent to "now, currently."

> *Dis   sapak   foo   ʔusa   dem   liif?*
> This SAPAC for where? them to-leave
> "Where have these women gone?"

dis: "this," general demonstrative.

sapak: from S.A.P.A.C., a popular brand of inexpensive dried cod; same slang meaning as in French.

ʔusa: "ou ça [where?]," but the dialect of Western Cameroon (on the former British side) has *hu-sayd* = "who + side."

dem: 3rd person plural selector.

liif: "leave"

Lingua francas with a more purely African character, such as Lingala, Sango, "Market Hausa," and "Up-Country Swahili," have many features in common with the trade languages having a European base, of which I have just given some examples: mixed vocabulary, simplified syntax reduced to a kind of common denominator in relationship to the local languages, irregular phonology, with multiple variations. The dividing line between African lingua francas and pidgins is sometimes difficult to lay down, as the two following sentences show:

> *Fita   nyu   aŋgadidɔŋ   befulis.*
> Whore this she-smooth-talked the policemen.

---

13. Examples borrowed from G. D. Schneider, personal communication (1960). The transcription adopted corresponds to the speech of Yaounde, from a Vute informant.

Dis   pita   i-don-didoŋ   dem pulis.
This whore she-smooth-talked them police.

The first is in "Popular Ewondo," or "truck-driver's Bulu"; the second is in Kos-Inglisi. Only the functional monemes, the morphemes, or tool-words, differ, while the nouns and verbs are the same:

> *fita/pita,* "whore," *didɔŋ, didoŋ,* "dis donc" ["say there"] (cf. *Irma la Douce*); *fulis/pulis,* "police," but:

dis: "this."

i-: "he/il," 3rd person singular selector.

-don-: "done," becomes the aspective of the completed past.

dem: "them," 3rd person plural selector.

nyu: Bulu, Ewondo, dependent nominal, nominal selector, cl. 1, CB *yu.*

a-: verbal prefix, cl. 1, CB *a-.*

-nga-: Bulu, Ewondo: *-ŋgá-,* morpheme of the general past.

be-: independent nominal prefix, cl. 2, CB *ba-.*

The first sentence is about as much Bulu as the following is English: "The *asée* of an *ntol mot* results from the *tye* of his *evú*"—which I fear I uttered in one of my classes. For the second sentence, I no longer dare have any opinion.

To construct a classification of African languages, one must gather the contemporary languages into groups within which each descends from a common ancestor language which has disappeared today; these groups are then gathered into branches, subfamilies, and families, still using the criterion of descent from a common ancestor language. The operation is a classic one and has been applied to Indo-European languages since the end of the eighteenth century and then to the Semitic languages. One important difference exists, however: while classical philology can rely on written documents dating back for several centuries, sometimes even several millennia, African linguists possess very few analogous documents, and these are of quite recent date. The process can thus produce only hypothetical reconstructions, which are often quite uncertain. To remain on solid ground, African linguistics must, then, rely on comparison of contemporary forms, for these are the only ones which are known with some certitude (and even this is not always true).

Comparison relies partly on the phonic shapes of words with the same meaning (or, for certain authors, similar or close meanings) and partly on the general structures, the grammatical mechanisms, of the languages to be compared. Depending on the school, the emphasis is stronger on one or the other aspect, but generally the modern tendency is to rely more and more heavily on comparative vocabularies.

Comparative vocabulary studies require certain precautions.[14] One must first isolate accidental resemblances: for example, the fact that in Bulu *ǹnóm* has the same meaning as "un homme" ("a man") in French does not at all prove that the two words descend from a common root. One must take into account the phonology of the two languages to be compared and the general shape of their words and then make a statistical calculation of the percentage beyond which there are only resemblances. In addition, particularly when dealing with geographically neighboring languages, or languages which have undergone similar cultural influences (Islam, colonization), one must isolate the loanwords borrowed from one language into the other or borrowed by both from a third language: the nouns */fudbol/*, */futbol/*, or */fotbal/*, which occur in French and Spanish, clearly do not descend from the common ancestor of these two languages, Latin. Similarly, the resemblance of *waziiri* in Hausa and *waziri* in Swahili proves nothing more than a common borrowing from Arabic.

Once these precautions have been taken, one may proceed to a comparison of words with identical meanings, preferably choosing concrete unambiguous notions and ones which are linked as little as possible to particular cultures or civilizations: body parts, common animals, numbers between one and ten, etc. At first sight, one might be tempted to retain only, or especially, those words in which the similarities leap to the eye. Things are unfortunately more complicated, for one must take into account both phonetic mutations, which occur in the course of time, and the phonological system of each language. This means, for example, that if one finds in language A, nine times out of ten, a $/p/$ where in language B there is an $/f/$, one would think that, in the tenth case where a $/p/$ in A corresponds to a $/p/$ in B, there is borrowing rather than common descent from a root ancestor.

The presentation of these comparisons may be made through the synoptic double-entry table like the one below, which I have borrowed from J. H. Greenberg ("Languages of Africa," p. 4).

Greenberg says:

> Even the first three words [columns] lead to a separation of these languages into two groups: I—1, 3, 6, 8; II—2, 4, 5, 7, which is confirmed by the other words [columns]. The two families are I. Saharan, II.

14. For more details see Joseph H. Greenberg, "The Languages of Africa," *International Journal of American Linguistics*, XXIX, No. 1 (January, 1963), pt. II (Indiana University Research Center in Anthropology, Folklore, and Linguistics Publication No. 25).

Niger-Congo. The languages are 1. Berti, 3. Teda, 6. Kanuri, 8. Zaghawa, 2. Kotopo (Adamawa), 4. Ahlŏ (Togo), 5. Proto-Bantu, 7. Efik. The addition of several hundred Niger-Congo languages and many additional words or grammatical forms would lend continuous further evidence for this same division.

	one	two	three	hand	eye	ear	mouth
1.	sang	● su	soti	yung	● sing	——	● a
2.	wate	■ iba	● tati	ju(le)	no(do)	● to(go)	yabodo
3.	● toro	● ču	agozo	● daho	● samo	■ sumo	■ či
4.	■ ili	■ iwa	● ita	ilɔ	ewu	● ɔtɔ	▲ ɛnu
5.	mwe	bali	● tato	■ (li)-to	(le)-iso	● (ku)-toi	▲ (mu)-nywa
6.	● tilo	ndi	yasko	kela	● sim	■ sumo	■ či
7.	kiet	■ iba	● ita	■ ɛte	enyin	● utong	▲ inua
8.	lakoi	● swe	we	● taha	i	kebbe	● a

This is only one small example. Tables used in practice contain one or two hundred columns and dozens of lines. Even this limited example shows, however, that the columns are not always homogeneous; that is, two words with identical meanings, belonging to the same family, may not present any resemblances. This fact has been used by the American linguist Swadesh to establish an equation which he believes allows one to calculate the chronological depth which separates two current languages from the date of their initial separation from the initial common language into two different speeches. Believing that the rate of change of the fundamental (basic) vocabulary is constant in all languages, he proposes the equation

$$t = \log C / 2 \log R,$$

where C is the proportion of words preserved in the basic vocabulary of the two languages, R is a "constant of retention" equal to about 0.81, and t is the minimal chronological depth of divergence, expressed in millennia.[15]

The validity of Swadesh's formula and its applicability to Africa are widely debated. This is unfortunate, since this formula would allow us to give absolute dates to the pre- and protohistorical migratory movements which simple comparative linguistics allows us to date in only a relative way, one by relationship to another.

Classic comparative linguistics was first systematically applied by Carl Meinhof to Bantu languages, whose strong homogeneity made them the perfect experimental ground. Meinhof, and later his successors, relied on the laws of historical Indo-European phonetics and extended

---

15. See D. H. Hymes, "Lexicostatistics So Far," *Current Anthropology*, I (Chicago: January, 1960).

them to Africa by analogy. Thus they attempted to reconstruct directly Urbantu, as spoken by the ancestors of present-day Bantu. In 1911, L. Homburger criticized Meinhof's method as being arbitrary and proposed a Common Bantu, which, like the one Guthrie proposed forty years later, represented more a common symbolization of modern forms than an exact reconstruction of ancestral forms, or the pretense of one. In the same year, Maurice Delafosse, proceeding largely on intuition, formulated the hypothesis of a common ancestor for Sudanic and Bantu languages, a hypothesis which eventually led him to propose the following classification for the languages of Africa:[16]

I. In the north and northeast, a large Hamito-Semitic family, extending as far as the Near East, of which the principal languages in Africa are Arabic, Berber, Amharic, and the Cushitic languages of Ethiopia and Somalia.

II. In the southwest, in the Kalahari and on its borders, the minuscule Hottentot-Bushman or Khoin family; at the turn of the century there was still a question whether it was related to the Hamito-Semitic group.

III. In all the rest of the continent, a large Negro-African family, including:

(a) on the one hand, the Bantu languages, which occupy a special place because of their homogeneity, their regularity, and—a point which has nothing to do with linguistics—the number of their speakers;

(b) on the other hand, the Sudano-Guinean languages, subdivided into 16 groups. For each of these I will give some typical languages:

1. *Nilo-Chadic*: Nuba, Baria, Kunama, Tubu, Tagali, Kadugli, Fur, Maba, Kanuri, Tama, Dajo, Zaghawa
2. *Nilo-Abyssinian*: Nuer, Dinka, Lwo, Didinga-Murle
3. *Nilo-Equatorial*: Maasai, Nandi, Kipsigis, Mbugu
4. *Kordofanian*: Tagoy, Talodi, Tumtum
5. *Nilo-Congolese*: Moru-Madi, Nyangbara, Lugbara, Mangbetu
6. *Ubangian*: Mungu-Mundu, Gbaya, Kredj, Sere, Zande, Barambo, Banda, Sango-Ngbandi, Manjia, Yangere, Mgbaka
7. *Chari-Waddaian*: Gula, Bongo, Kaba, Barma, Mbrak
8. *Charian*: Somraï, Miltu, Bwa
9. *Nigero-Chadic*: Buduma, Kotoko, Musgu, Mandara, Margi, Jarawa, Hausa

16. V. A. Meillet and M. Cohen, eds., *Les langues du monde*, 2d ed. (Paris, 1948). There is a good résumé of the theses of Delafosse and Westermann in Th. Monod, *L'Hippopotame et le philosophe*, 2d ed. (Paris, 1946), chap. 15.

10. *Nigero-Cameroonian*: Jukun, Tiv, Vute, Tikar, Nupe, Efik, Igbo, Yoruba
11. *Lower-Nigerian*: Ijaw
12. *Voltaic*:[17] Bariba, Tem; More; Dagari-Birifor; Gurunsi; Lobi; Kulango; Bobo; Senufo
13. *Eburno-Dahomean*: Ewe; Kposo; Gã, Guang; Twi-Akan; "Apollonien"; "Agni"; "Lagunaire"
14. *Nigero-Senegalese*: Jerma-Songhaï; Dogon-Busanka; Sarakole-Ajer; "Mandingo": "Mande-Tan" (Bambara, Dyula, Kono, Vai), "Mande-Fu" (Tura, Guro, Kpele, Mende, Susu)
15. *Eburno-Liberian*: Bete; Kru-Basa; Grebo
16. *Senegalo-Guinean*: Fulani; Wolof; Serer-Non; Serer-Sin; Balante; Basari-Konyagi; Kisi; Temne, Bulom, Krim

This classification was solidly grounded for the languages of extreme West Africa—the French West African Federation of the period—which Delafosse knew well, since he had lived there for a long time as an administrator. It was less well grounded for Equatorial Africa, where he had only traveled, and much less so for Central and Nilotic Africa, whose languages he knew only indirectly, through second-hand documents—usually very brief ones. Even for West Africa, however, some of his decisions are debatable. Later research proved him correct on such points as the attachment of Fulani to the Negro-African family and on the over-all composition of the Voltaic group (12). On the other hand, his classification of Songhaï with "Mandingo" (Nigero-Senegalese group, 14) has been disproved, while the question of Hausa (Nigero-Chadic, 9) remains very controversial.

Diedrich Westermann also believed in the common origin of the Bantu and Sudanic languages. In 1940 he published, in *Völkerkunde von Afrika* (French translation: *Les peuples et civilisations de l'Afrique* [Paris, 1948]), a classification quite different from Delafosse's. Westermann's was based on a more complete and precise documentation and used morphological and structural arguments as often as, and sometimes more frequently than, lexical and phonetical arguments (for which Greenberg criticizes him). Westermann's first classification confirms most of Delafosse's hypotheses for West Africa but differs radically from his conclusions about the rest of the continent. Westermann's classification is as follows:

I. HAMITO-SEMITIC, subdivided into:
  1. SEMITIC

17. The semicolons separate the subgroups.

2. HAMITIC: (a) Berber-Libyan; (b) Cushitic; (c) unclassified languages of East Africa, having common characteristics with Khoi-San

II. KHOI-SAN, subdivided into:
  1. SAN (Bushman), with three groups, South, Central, and North
  2. KHOI (Hottentot), with two groups, of which the northern one is related to the "unclassified languages of East Africa" mentioned above

III. NEGRO LANGUAGES, a large family divided into three branches:
  1. BANTU
  2. SUDANIC, with four sections:
     (2) A: *Semi-Bantu*: with ten groups, partially corresponding to groups 4, 10, 12, 13, and 16 of Delafosse. This concerns languages with more or less complete class systems. The main groups are:[18]
       W III—2A—3, "Benue–Cross River" (D 10), including Tiv and the languages of the Bamileke plateaus of Cameroon
       W III—2A—8, "Gur" (D 12), virtually identical to the "Voltaic" of Delafosse
       W III—2A—9, "West Atlantic" (D 16), with three subgroups and excluding Fulani, which is classified separately (W III—2A—10)
     (2) B: *Nigritic*: with 17 groups, covering or cutting into D 1, 5, 6, 10, and 14, more or less. Nigritic extends from the Niger Valley (W III—2B—17 [D 14]) to the valleys of the Nile, to the east (Nuba, W III—2B—3 [D 1]), and Ubangi, to the south (W III—2B—6 to 13 [D 5 and 6])
     (2) C: *Mandingo* (D 14), divided into two groups, Mande-Tan and Mande-Fu, whose names but not contents are the same as in Delafosse
     (2) D: *Hinterland Sudan*, corresponding, *grosso modo*, with the Chad Basin, with seven groups and numerous subgroups, containing a part of the languages of D 1, 7, 8, and 9. The group W III—2D—7 is called "Hausa-Kotoko."
  3. NILOTIC: family (or branch) not foreseen by Delafosse, with four groups:
     (3) A: *Nilo-Sudanese*, containing most of the languages D 2
        B: *Nilo-Hamitic*, generally D 3

18. The cross-references to the various classifications will henceforth be coded D for Delafosse, W for Westermann, G for Greenberg, followed by a number or a reference symbol.

C: *Didinga-Murle* (D 2)
D: *Dar Fung* (D 2)

This classification is the only over-all classification Westermann published during his lifetime. When it appeared, he was already beginning to revise it, an undertaking which he continued until his death. He collaborated with his colleagues at the School of Oriental and African Studies in London. The first volume was published in 1952 in collaboration with Miss M. A. Bryan[19] and modified partially the classification of West African languages, redistributing them into eight homogeneous groups: West Atlantic (reintegrating Fulani into this), Mande, Songhaï, Kru, Kwa, Chadic, and Chado-Hamitic (including Hausa), plus two catchall heterogeneous groups: languages without classes, languages with classes (these latter two including a good part of the previous "Semi-Bantu").

After Westermann's death, A. N. Tucker and M. A. Bryan, working in his spirit and with his techniques, succeeded in revising his classification of the languages of Central and Nilotic Africa.[20] Their work proposes ten "larger units" and twenty-four "isolated" groups, or languages. The "larger units" include as many "Nigritic" languages (Bongo-Bagirmi [D 7], Moru-Mangbetu [D 5], Sere-Mundu [D 6], Zande [D 6], Banda-Gbaya-Ngbandi [D 6], East Saharan [D 1], and Koalib-Tagoi [D 4]) as "Nilotic" (Nilotic [D 2], Nilo-Hamitic [D 3])—and even "Hamito-Semitic" ones (Cushitic; absent in Delafosse). The former "languages without classes in East Africa" are definitively inked to the "Khoi-San."

On the whole, then, the Anglo-German classification, or the revised classification of Westermann, tends to be more synthetic than its predecessors with regard to the languages of West Africa, but, on the contrary, to be rather less synthetic when it comes to the languages of Central Africa or of the Northeast. At the same time that this revision was being made, the United States made a shattering entry into the domain of African linguistics with the publication of *Studies in African Linguistic Classification* by J. H. Greenberg in 1955.

This work was much less revolutionary than was thought at the time (especially in the United States), except perhaps for the violence with which the author attacked both his predecessors and contemporaries. The Bantuists, and Bantu, came under particularly heavy attack. Greenberg proclaimed, or rather claimed, with some semblance of

19. D. Westermann and M. A. Bryan, *Handbook of African Languages*, II: *Languages of West Africa* (London, 1952).
20. Tucker and Bryan, *The Non-Bantu Languages of North-Eastern Africa* (London, 1956).

correctness, that if Bantu was as closely linked to Sudanic languages as they thought it was, there was no reason to make it a separate family. As for "Semi-Bantu," this was a term as idiotic and with as little justification as "Semi-French" applied to Italian would be, or "Semi-English" applied to German. The classification which he proposed—sometimes with rather flimsy arguments—displayed the same tendency as the revised Westermann classification: it was less synthetic than its predecessors and tended toward a greater number of families (and thus of prehistoric ancestor languages). One might particularly criticize this work because of its tone, a tone which gained it a *succès de scandale* rather than a scientific success, a fact which has in itself hurt the second classification presented by Greenberg.

This second classification was *Languages of Africa*, published in 1963, which represents a return to a high-level synthetic classification of the languages of Africa. Most linguists who did not quarrel with Greenberg after his first work (and some of those who did) now accept the major part of his new classification, finding fault with only a few rather minor details. This classification is as follows:

I. A large CONGO-KORDOFANIAN family, partially covering the "Negro-African" family of Delafosse and the "Negro" family of Westermann and divided into:
   I—A. Niger-Congo branch, with the groups:
      1. West Atlantic (D 16; W III—2A—9)
      2. Mande (D 14; W III—2C)
      3. Voltaic (D 12; W III—2B—8)
      4. Kwa (D 10, 11, 13, 15; W III—2B—18 to 23)
      5. Benue-Congo (Bantu! + D 10; W III—2A—1 to 5)
      6. Adamawa (D 6; W III—2D)
   I—B. Kordofanian branch (D 4 and various others)

II. A NILO-SAHARAN family, with six branches:
   II—A. Songhaï (D 14; W III—2B—17)
   II—B. Saharan (D 1; W III—2D—3)
   II—E. Chari-Nile (D 1, 2; W III—2B—1 to 6 and W 3—1 to 3)

III. An AFRO-ASIATIC family—the "Hamito-Semitic" of other authors—with five branches:
   III—E. Chad, to which Hausa is linked (D 9; W III—2D—7), an opinion already held in France from the end of the nineteenth century but which remains debatable

IV. The KHOI-SAN family, with three branches

It is Greenberg's classification which I have used for the map on page 71. Although I do not entirely share his opinions on points such as the classification of Hausa in the Afro-Asiatic family or certain details about the languages of Cameroon, I still feel that, given the actual state of our knowledge, it is not possible to group the Negro-African ensemble of Delafosse into a single group, that is, to postulate a common ancestor for Greenberg's two families, Niger-Kordofanian and Nilo-Saharan. This situation may well change within a few years, if more systematic and more in-depth studies are undertaken on Nilotic Central Africa, where the languages are still very little known—barely explored, in fact. A. N. Tucker and M. A. Bryan, for example, have just discovered indications in this region which lead one to believe in the existence of a "t/k substratum" which seems common to the Afro-Asiatic languages as well as some of the Niger-Kordofanian and Nilo-Saharan. Such a discovery, if it were confirmed, could upset many theories about the genesis of Semitic languages and the movements of prehistoric populations between Africa and the Near East.

Basing himself on the first works of Greenberg, his colleague and compatriot G. P. Murdock has recently formulated a new hypothesis on the genesis of African populations.[21] According to him, a Negro Neolithic agricultural civilization was formed in the valley of the Middle Niger and spread first toward the east, where, by fusing with pastoral peoples from the Near East, this civilization gave birth to the predynastic Egyptian civilization. Another branch, descending into the south and installing itself in the present Nigerian-Cameroonian border mountains, launched a movement into the forest in a south and south-westerly direction, from the sixth century of our era, and became the source of the Bantu population in southern and equatorial Africa.

Unfortunately, the main opponent of J. H. Greenberg, Malcolm Guthrie of London, also on the basis of extremely convincing linguistic evidence, arrives at a completely different understanding of Bantu origins. According to Guthrie, the Bantu ancestors left the Chad-Cameroonian confines and followed the valleys of the Logone, Chari, Sangha, and the Congo to install themselves at the sources of the Congo, near Lake Mweru, where their descendants later split into two groups, western and eastern, each group then diffusing to both the north and the south. The Bantoid traits actually observed in many West African languages would be due to the infiltration of much less

---

21. G. P. Murdock, *Africa: Its Peoples and Their Culture History* (New York, 1959).

Map 2. — A Sketch of Language Families in Africa

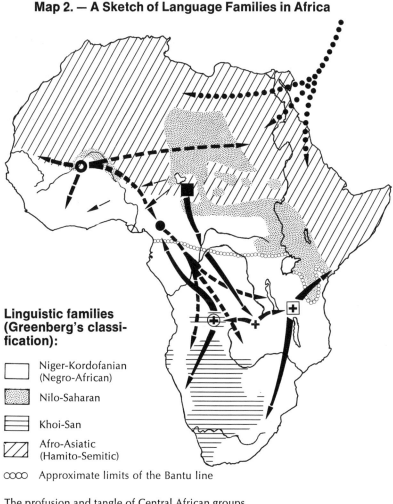

Linguistic families (Greenberg's classification):

☐ Niger-Kordofanian (Negro-African)

▨ Nilo-Saharan

☷ Khoi-San

▨ Afro-Asiatic (Hamito-Semitic)

ΟΟΟΟ Approximate limits of the Bantu line

The profusion and tangle of Central African groups has been greatly simplified:

■ Departure point of the Pre-Bantu

✚ Proto-Bantu homeland, according to Guthrie

⊕ Western Proto-Bantu

⊞ Eastern Proto-Bantu

◄ ▬ Migrations of the Pre-Bantu and the Bantu (Guthrie)

◄ — Diffusion of Pre-Bantu elements in (West) Africa

◄ ▬▬ African migrations, according to Murdock

◯ Neolithic homeland of Sudanic agriculture

● Proto-Bantu homeland, according to Greenberg

◄ ●● Asiatic stock-breeders (Proto-Semites)

important groups which left for the west at various dates, independently of the principal migratory wave.

It is extremely difficult to make an objective choice between these two theories, which are equally appealing and equally confirmed, or contradicted, by concrete proofs, particularly archaeological ones.[22] In my opinion the two theories are partially reconcilable, since there must have existed permanent routes of exchange and migration involving secondary interferences which complicate and falsify overly simplified schemas; also, we know very little about the sociology of linguistic contacts in Africa and the factors which hinder or help the spread of unwritten languages. The important point, and what I hope to emphasize here, is the importance that this kind of linguistic palaeontology has for reconstructing the past of peoples without writing. Obviously these techniques need to be refined and made more explicit, and the results need to be compared with other kinds of studies. Linguistics nevertheless continues to provide an absolutely indispensable golden thread.

22. Guthrie's theory undoubtedly meshes better with the Bantu facts, but only with these. Greenberg's theory, appealing because of its generality, is perhaps still a bit premature, given the facts available to us. Once again, then, we see the need for increasing the number of monographs.

CHAPTER IV

From Tribes to Nations: Problems of Communication

Past linguistic sociology: the precolonial period, conquests and migrations. The Pygmy mystery. Bantu "race," "Hamitic culture": no! Early contacts with Europe: from slave dealers to explorers.

Recent linguistic sociology: the colonial period. Colonial attitudes toward African languages: François I and Robespierre *vs.* Lord Lugard and indirect rule on questions of education. Theories and realities.

Present linguistic sociology: African emancipation follows in the footsteps of colonialism. The language of nationalism resorts to "colonial" languages. Cultural decolonization and technical requirements: equal pulls in opposite directions. Toward the birth of a language proletariat? Theoretical solutions and possible compromises. Factors of choice: the situation of various states in terms of linguistic homogeneity. Social change and language adaptivity. The unreal problem of the π meson. Problems of translating political ideas. Electronics to the rescue.

Future linguistic sociology: the author refuses to prophesy. Attempts at extrapolation: for the "colonial" languages: toward the dialectalization of French and English? African languages: the larger ones will destroy the smaller ones. Electronics again, linked to the world-wide primary-produce market.

We know virtually nothing about the linguistic sociology of precolonial Africa, which is often a nuisance, since we attempt to base our reconstructions of migratory movements on the spread and breakdown of current languages. A tendency too often seen consists in envisioning African migrations much as the Bible depicts the Exodus of the children of Israel: whole groups progressing in tight columns and submerging or driving off the inhabitants wherever they pass. There may well have been migrations of this type—oral tradition indicates a few—but, at least as often, the migrants functioned as small groups of well-armed warriors, settling in a distant village by force of arms or by trickery and founding families there, after massacring or enslaving the male inhabitants and after marrying their wives, sisters, daughters, or widows—or at least getting them pregnant. Oral traditions also show cases of this kind, often in the form of legends recounting the amorous and martial exploits of a single heroic ancestor.

What happened during these population movements? In some cases, a huge migration must have been accompanied by the diffusion of the migrants' language, which replaced that of the conquered or of those groups who were pushed back. On the other hand, a small group of adventurers might have usurped power in the midst of the foreigners, whose language they then adopted, while also preserving part of the terminology, especially the political and religious terminology, of their own homeland. In still other cases, invasion or conquest may have resulted in the coexistence of several languages used by different classes in the population. An example of the first type would be the diffusion in South Africa of the Nguni group (Zulu, Xhosa) which have themselves been influenced by the languages of the conquered populations (Bushmen and Hottentots). The reverse situation obtains among the aristocracy of Gurma origin, in the Kotokoli kingdom of Northern Togo, who adopted the language (Tem) of the conquered groups. Among the Fulani chieftaincies of Northern Cameroon, especially, one finds a situation of coexistence. There Fulfulde coexists with the languages of populations conquered in the nineteenth century.

The degree to which African languages are resistant or fragile ties in not only with the political ups-and-downs of the society where the languages are spoken but, even more, with obvious demographic factors (languages which become extinct for lack of speakers, etc.) and with other variables which are not always so easily discerned. Kikongo, for instance, has changed very little since the seventeenth century, while a neighboring language, Ifumu, described by a missionary in 1911, has completely disappeared only a half-century later. There is also the Pygmy mystery, for we still do not know whether they have or have had a specific language. Generally, bands of Pygmies speak languages which differ, sometimes very fundamentally, from those of the Blacks with whom they live in a virtual state of socioeconomic symbiosis. Until now each of the so-called Pygmy languages which has been recorded has turned out to be an authentic Black African language, closely related to the languages of Blacks living at substantial distances from the actual settlement of the Pygmies in question. This might indicate either that these Pygmies have moved or—and this appears to be the more frequent case—that their one-time and ancient Black neighbors[1] have migrated, while they themselves have remained in the same place.[2]

The only general affirmation which can confidently be put forward about the situation in precolonial Africa is that there was almost never an exact coincidence of physical type, language, and civilization. The most notable exception (there always have to be exceptions!) is that of the Bushmen of the Kalahari, among whom a specific physical type, a unique civilization, and a special language coexist. We must, however, point out that this physical type is partially shared by the Hottentots, that certain aspects of their civilization exist among the steppe hunters of northeast Africa, and that their language has influenced that of Bantu invaders and probably also that of the Hottentots. Everywhere else, the frequent identification of a language or a family of languages, a civilization, and a physical type are abuses of speech or scientific errors, if not political maneuvers. Thus there is NO "Bantu type" or "Bantu civilization." The word "Bantu" should not and cannot be applied honestly except to a language family (or a subgroup, if we take Greenberg's classification). There is no Bantu physical type: the Beye'ele Pygmies of the Cameroon speak a Bantu language, as do the gigantic Watutsi of Rwanda. There is no "Bantu matriarchy": the Fang of the northwest and the Zulu of the southeast are patrilineal and speak Bantu languages; the Ashanti of Ghana are matrilineal and speak Kwa.

The same holds true for the so-called "Hamites": the Fulani of West Africa speak a Negro-African language (or Niger-Kordofanian) from the West Atlantic group (or Senegalo-Guinean); the Tutsi of Rwanda and Burundi also speak a Niger-Kordofanian language (or Negro-

1. The distinction which certain Anglo-Saxon anthropologists make between "Blacks" and "Bantu" is generally rejected by the French school, which postulates instead a general type, "Negro" or "Negro African," geographically differentiated. Despite this, the Pygmies correspond to a very distinct physical type, truly to another race. (I still hesitate to use the last word, because of the atrocious misuses to which it is still put.)

2. A very recent botanical investigation, as yet unpublished, seems to prove that the botanical terminology of the Pygmies of Ituri (Congo-Kinshasa) greatly resembles that of the Pygmies in East Cameroon, although the two languages differ widely on every other point. If this new fact is confirmed by deeper investigations, we may possibly be on the way to finding a true Pygmy linguistic substratum.

African) from the Bantu group (or the Benue-Congo group). Neither are Hamites, although both have great esteem for longhorn cattle,[3] a taste which they share with the Masai of Kenya and Tanganyika. The Masai are Nilo-Hamites, according to Westermann, but according to Greenberg they belong to the eastern Sudanic groups of the Nilo-Saharan family, which connects them with the Songhaï and the Kanuri but not at all with the Berbers.

After the second half of the nineteenth century, colonial intervention upset the sociology of Africa, in the linguistic sphere as in all others. Except during the first decades following the Portuguese discoveries, linguistic contacts were definitely minimal in the preimperialist phase of European action in Africa. The slave traders generally negotiated with the African dealers along the coast through a "language master" as go-between. These men were often of mixed blood and learned French, English, Dutch, or Portuguese in the various ports and, more rarely, on board ships. These they learned well enough to be able to serve as interpreters and nothing more. The formation of coastal pidgins probably dates from this era and from this type of relations. Rare were the Europeans who learned African languages. Since missionary activity had been virtually paralyzed by the slave trade from the mid-seventeenth century onwards, recruitment of linguist-priests had dried up. As for those few European traders who were sufficiently permanently established to learn an African language, most became acculturated to the point of becoming founders of completely Africanized families, some of which, recognizable by Latin or Anglo-Saxon family names, still count among the aristocracy or upper class of the coast.

Once the penetration of the interior had begun in earnest, the first explorers sought interpreters either among the coastal peoples who were accustomed to trading with peoples of the interior, or among natives of the interior regions, many of whom, sold as slaves to illegal slave dealers, had been liberated by the British naval squadron suppressing slavery and resettled in European bases (Freetown, Goree, Libreville), often at considerable distances from their homes. In many cases these interpreters had only the most rudimentary knowledge of the language of their employers, who thus were often obliged to learn one or several African languages, a practice which continued and became official policy in the British, German, and Belgian colonial systems, although not in the French.[4]

3. I prefer to pass in silence over the name of a famous German linguist who based his linguistic groupings on the forms of cattle horns.
4. The Portuguese system is unique because of the important role which mixed-blood groups and bilingual Creoles played over a long period of time.

The slave trade had posed hardly any problems of communication: a common language with the people who were bought to be resold was not a necessity. The problem arose only for the purchaser, on the other side of the Atlantic. With colonization, however, it became essential to communicate as directly as possible with the colonized population, especially if the goal was to transform social, political, economic, and religious institutions.

Two diametrically opposed solutions were either to impose exclusive use of the conquering language as quickly as possible or, on the contrary, to have the representatives of the conquering power use local languages exclusively. These are, of course, only theoretical solutions, since their application would in any case have presupposed some linguistic exchange, if only to collect the information necessary for carrying them out. In practice, Europeans tended toward one or the other according to the implications of their explicit colonial policy and the position they occupied in this system. The Anglo-Germanic powers tended toward the use of local languages, the Latin powers toward diffusion of their own languages. In a similar way, higher officials, members of the official or commercial bureaucracy, did not have the same requirements or the same opportunities of direct contact with the indigenous people as did the territorial administrators, missionaries, or small traders; their attitudes toward local languages and the teaching of European languages could thus differ greatly.

French colonial policy on education and administration can be easily defined: it is the creation of François I, Richelieu, Robespierre, and Jules Ferry. Only one language is taught in the schools, recognized in law courts, and used in administration: French, as defined by the opinions of the Academy and the decrees of the minister of public education. All other languages belong to the realm of folklore, dancing around the maypole, and riding hobbyhorses and are signs of disintegration of the French Republic. Such at least were the principles concretely underlying the decrees of the 1930's, which forbade the use in teaching, even in private education, of any language other than French (except for catechism and religious instruction, fields outside official sanction). In practice the decree was probably never completely followed: the marines used Bambara for teaching regiments of Senegalese *tirailleurs*[5] until it was realized that it was probably easier to let Corsican privates, Alsatian sergeants, or Breton corporals use French to teach a right-about-face to the Mossi, Lobi, or Sara recruits. Administrators were encouraged by minimal bonuses to learn local languages, in order to be able to check on the veracity of their interpreters (but, as soon as they

5. So named because they were generally recruited outside Senegal.

learned one, there was always a governor who transferred them, fearing they might gain too much personal influence over the populations they administered). The lack of means, the very size of Africa, not to mention the fear that certain people shared of seeing education "corrupt the natives"—all these factors hindered the spread of the French language. By its very rarity, French remained an element of social prestige, not for itself as much as for the opportunities it offered; and public opinion played in favor of its spread: the parents of children in missionary schools particularly demanded, even before the administration entered the scene, that mission schools stop teaching in local languages and teach in French.

Only the Islamized populations, often with a centuries-long background of education and initiated into writing and scholarly teaching, showed some opposition to French schools, for these seemed to them to threaten the teaching of Arabic, the religious language. Now and then there were cases where Muslim chiefs, summoned by the "commandant" to recruit students, filled the schools with sons of slaves or with children belonging to pagan groups scorned by the Muslims, never suspecting that, a generation later, these same children, having become political leaders thanks to these accidental benefits, would put an end to the last vestiges of power of those who had thus involuntarily set them on the path of progress.

On the level of linguistics, this education given exclusively in French had various results. On the one side was the incompatability between attendance at school and customary traditional education, which, contrary to what we too often think, included a real language training, particularly in rhetoric and occasionally in the traditional poetry: a negative factor, then, relative to the preservation of the art of the spoken word and to a purist conservatism, which causes numerous elders today to bemoan the fact that their children "no longer speak their language." On the other side, since they were left to themselves, these languages were not frozen by a more or less well-adapted transcription[6] and thus remained free to evolve at their own speed and to adapt themselves with suppleness to the demands of changing social contexts. In particular, the absence of writing and of fixed, obligatory "school-dialect" forms permitted in some cases the fusion into one single language of dialects or neighboring speech patterns which had remained

---

6. I recently had a rather unpleasant surprise when I wanted to investigate the language of an African student in Paris. I found that he spoke what one may call a seminary dialect, that is, a language as it was pronounced by European missionaries reading an incorrect transcription, and not the language that was spoken in the villages.

differentiated by the difficulty of communication. This can be considered a positive factor.

If it is partially true that the French educational policy resulted from a definite cultural imperialism (and from a definite Malthusianism working in favor of quality at the expense of quantity), it is no less true that the same policy came from an equal amount of humane generosity, doubtless ethnocentric and nationalistic, but generosity nevertheless. Since the Frenchman was the standard for universal man (like Breteuil's standard meter of platinum), and his language was *the* language, France was offering the Africans everything that was best in culture, in the whole of mankind. In truth, *the* Culture.

Conversely, the marked respect which the British and Germans showed for African languages and institutions probably included certain feelings of intrinsic superiority, or rather incommunicable privilege: "Niggers begin at Calais," and it takes two centuries to grow a British lawn or to integrate oneself into "this happy breed of men." Among the Belgians, however (and probably also in Kenya and the Rhodesias), the exclusive use of African languages for education and administration resulted incontestably from the desire to keep the Africans in a kind of linguistic prison or, if one prefers, to shelter them and keep them sheltered from dangerous reading (neither Voltaire nor Marx has been translated into "government" Kikongo). The same fact applies to the recent decision of the South African government to use Bantu languages in schools.

In many cases, such decisions often encounter a serious difficulty: which language or languages should be chosen? It is quite impossible in countries with great linguistic diversity to use all the local languages in education or administration, if only because of economic or other material considerations. A choice has to be made, based on various factors. In some cases a local language obviously occupies a privileged position as the commercial, religious, or political language; the colonizers had then only to notice this and take it into account; generally such languages are found at the level of a province, and too much generalization from this is dangerous. In another favorable case, several languages may be closely enough related so that one among them may be chosen and developed into a koinē; this, however, presupposes an intimate prior understanding of the language situation.

In many cases the choice has resulted from an accident: one language may have received an official character because a missionary had established a relatively complete dictionary or grammar, or because an administrative post had, for reasons of climate, been set up in a certain language zone, or because a language appeared to be the easiest one to teach to European officials.[7] One result was to make a speaker of A language teach B language to children of C, D, and E languages (for example: in Uganda, a Lwo teacher taught Swahili to Lugbara children —and the three languages were not even related). Eventually this is what happened in the French colonies, except that the teaching language, B, had a universal spread and was not simply tribal or regional. In other words, instead of making an arbitrary choice of a "foreign" local language for education and for official purposes, why not use English or French? Particularly since, indirect rule or not, the British colonial system, just as much as the French, necessitated the use of English-speaking African agents, if only to type the reports of the District Officers to His Excellency the Governor & C. in C. Thus there was both a persuasive reason for knowing English and a widespread desire to learn it. The primary school only partially satisfied this demand, and that in the last years of school (if the child got that far); moreover, English was not used as the *language of instruction* but was rather taught as a *subject*. In West Africa the result was a higher school enrollment in British colonies but a knowledge of English which was definitely inferior to the knowledge of French in French colonies. On the whole, we may say that the French spoken by a Togolese schoolchild who received his certificate of primary schooling was equal or superior to the English of his cousins who passed the secondary-school exams (GCE) in the Gold Coast. A balancing factor was the existence in British Africa of a relatively abundant vernacular literature, and many country folk who did not know a word of English could nevertheless read and write in their own language. Besides, and especially, where education was given in the mother tongue, or a close relative of it, there was not the huge gap between family and village life and school life which proved so wasteful in the French colonial school system.

The school system was not the only factor involved in this. British administrators were supposed to learn an African language during their first tour of duty and to remain throughout most of their career in the region where that language was spoken. French administrators rarely spent more than two years in the same region and, unless they were

7. Among the four official languages of the Congo were "simplified Kikongo" or "government Kikongo," "basic Chiluba," and "Kiswahili Kingwana," languages which, according to a caustic Congolese, were "reduced to the basic mental level of a simplified average Flemish government official." On the other hand, it is equally true that a grammar of "literary Lingala" was published, which is Lingala as it should be instead of Lingala as it is. This in no way detracts from the quality of the linguistic works published by Belgian linguists in the Congo, for they definitely are the leaders in all studies of this kind in the French language.

bachelors, were often regarded suspiciously by their superiors or colleagues if they spoke or tried to speak the language of the people they administered.[8] Everything actually revolved around the interpreter,[9] and the desire to bypass his obligatory mediation sufficed to convince many peasants to send their children to school. In any official capacity, even the lowest one, a knowledge of French was essential—and it was expected to be French, not a pidgin French. Contrary to what one sees in Rhodesia and South Africa, a good knowledge of the language of the colonial dominators was not considered symptomatic of a subversive mentality at all. Quite the opposite. Finally, the mixture resulting from civil and military recruitment, mixing the ethnic groups in batallions and in labor groups, under the command of a metropolitan noncommissioned officer or foreman, further contributed to making French a pan-African language. This fact had great importance at the time of independence.

It is striking to note that independent Africa is presently divided into "English-speaking Africa" and "French-speaking Africa." These two phrases generate particularly dangerous illusions,[10] for I do not believe that the number of Africans able to express themselves effectively in these two languages surpasses 10 per cent of the *total* population.

The fact nevertheless remains that French and English, immediately followed by Arabic, are the principal languages of Black Africa, not so much because of the number of their speakers—who are probably fewer in number than Swahili-speakers—but by the quality of their language and the high-ranking social and economic positions they occupy. Indeed, these three languages—two Indo-European and one Semitic —are the most useful tools, truly indispensable instruments, for any political or ideological creation at the pan-African level. French is, to a certain extent, privileged in this sense, for, although probably spoken by fewer people, it is more uniformly distributed in space and penetrates the masses more deeply: a schoolteacher in Dakar can use it to discuss things with his colleague from Bangui, while a Yoruba schoolteacher

8. We must not forget, however, that Delafosse, Vieillard, Gaden, and Labouret, to cite only those who have died, were administrators and that until World War II the great majority of serious works on Africa were written by administrators, missionaries, and colonial army personnel; academic Africanist studies only began appearing in the 1930's, led by the team of Griaule, Weulersse, Monod, Leiris, et al.

9. By the curious logic of the French administrative system, civil service interpreters were interpreters per se in the sense that, almost as mobile as European officials, they were sent everywhere, even into regions where they did not know the language.

10. I have recently read that "Black Africa has forty-five million French-speakers." If such be the case, there would be at least a hundred million anglosaxophones, as a UNESCO official called the English-speaking (anglophonic) Africans.

in Western Nigeria may have no common language with an Ibo colleague in Eastern Nigeria.

Linguistic arguments played a very minor role in anticolonial movements before and after World War II. Several events have proven this: the reactions of the Ganda and of the Kikuyu against the use of Swahili in schools before World War II; the agitation in favor of an "Eweland," regrouping the Ewe of Ghana and Togo, from 1946 to 1950; or the projects aiming at reconstructing the Kongo empire, which are still discussed on both sides of the Pool. Each of these is a case of tribal demands as much as, or more than, national ones. No matter how artificial the colonial partition of the nineteenth century was, the boundaries it established have acquired a sociological reality; and disputing these boundaries with the intention of showing greater consideration for ethnic or linguistic units would now create more problems than it would resolve. Indeed, the only practical end which African languages have served during the political developments of the past few years has been to act as secret codes in certain insurrectionist movements. At the trial of Jomo Kenyatta, for instance, the defense attacked lengthily and violently the translations of Kikuyu documents provided by the Kenyan anthropologist Leakey, discoverer of Zinjanthropus man at Olduvai Gorge, the oldest known human fossil. In Cameroon, the guerilla "bush-fighters" of Sanaga-Maritime (a "bush" of thirty-meter-high trees!) corresponded in Basa, a language unknown to the French police forces. Throughout most of Africa, the propaganda in vernacular or local languages, where translations lacked the nuances, was much more violent than propaganda put forth in French or English; this stems particularly from semantic reasons, to which I shall return.

Various intellectual groups posed the question of "linguistic decolonization," particularly in Paris within the group called the African Society of Culture. This discussion often lacked realism, largely because most of the participants had no idea of general linguistics and even less of African linguistics.[11]

A small group from the Left Bank thus bravely proposed the adoption of a "national language of Africa": "Common Negro-African." This astonished the linguists, who, as stated above, are far from being able to give a credible reconstruction of such a language. On further examination, this group avowed that "Common Negro-African" was no other than classical Greek, "stolen from Africa by the colonialists." The theory nevertheless retains some supporters, primarily recruited from the ranks of people knowing neither Greek nor African languages.

11. Nevertheless, there are some excellent African linguists: President L. S. Senghor, whose student I am proud to have been, to give only one example.

A much more serious and rational argument is that put forth and adopted during the Second Congress of Black Writers and Artists, which met in Rome in 1958. The linguistic resolution adopted by this Congress[12] foresaw the adoption of an important contemporary African language and its obligatory use as a lingua franca throughout the continent. Difficulties arose when the language had to be chosen, and the Congress had to be content with giving a list of "possibilities": Swahili, Hausa, Yoruba, Mande, Fulfulde, and Wolof. Significantly, only the last two belong to the same group (West Atlantic), and the others are either distantly or not at all related. In such conditions—quite apart from the nationalist reactions and the material difficulties which implementation of this resolution would imply—there would scarcely be any improvement in the problems of teaching or in the ease of learning: Yoruba, for example, would be as difficult as English for a Kenyan or a Tanzanian to learn. Evidently the supporters of this resolution, having little acquaintance with the specific scientific meaning of language relationships, built up an overoptimistic idea of the actual resemblances between Negro-African languages and the teaching ease offered by them. The theory is that since French, Spanish, German, Russian, and Indian students learn English well, there is nothing absurd about the idea of a Senegalese, Ghanaian, Malian, or Guinean student learning a language such as Swahili—except that its practical usefulness is much smaller than that of French, English, Russian, or German.

French, English, Russian, and German: it happens to be true that, in this second half of the twentieth century, these four languages, especially the first two, are the only international languages of technical and scientific cultures and that knowledge of at least two of them may be considered indispensable for any scientist or advanced technician who wants to "remain in the race." It is not widely known that the scientists of such advanced nations as Holland, the Scandinavian countries, Czechoslovakia, or Poland publish in these four languages as much as or more than in their own. History has resulted in the accidental wide diffusion of two of these languages, English and French, in present-day modern Africa, and therein lies, in my opinion, one of the main contributions made by the colonial era, insofar as knowledge of a technical language is indispensable to economic or social development. Certainly, the third international language which is widespread in Africa, Arabic, enjoys a popularity comparable to French, but it is not—or it is no longer—the language of a technical culture; its profitability on the scientific level actually is less than that of Spanish or Portuguese (but

12. Summary and Proceedings in *Présence Africaine*, nos. 24–25 and 27–28 (February–May and August–November, 1959).

probably equal or superior to that of the Afrikaaners' Taal). In terms of immediate practical utility, then, it is in the best interests of the independent African states to work on the basis of this positive colonial legacy and to develop the use of French and English.[13]

Such is the solution adopted by all of the emancipated states. Only three—Northern Nigeria, Tanganyika, and Zanzibar—have decided to give a local language national status: Hausa in Northern Nigeria and Swahili in Tanganyika and Zanzibar. They have, however, preserved the use of English,[14] which is, for example, the federal language of Nigeria. Mauritania—which belongs only very marginally to Black Africa—has also kept French as the official language, along with Arabic. Shortly before the assassination of President Olympio, Togo had decided to use Ewe, and Hausa secondarily, as official languages conjointly with French, but this decision does not seem to have been carried out. Finally, the Federal Republic of Cameroon has chosen as official languages both English and French.[15]

The teaching of English and French has also been quantitatively reinforced everywhere, sometimes at the expense of quality. In most of the former British colonies, English is taught as a subject starting in the third year of primary school and is the language of instruction during the last two years; French has been introduced as a foreign language (usually optional) in many secondary schools in Sierra Leone, Ghana, and Nigeria. In the former French colonies, primary education has always been in French, and English was a compulsory subject in secondary schools. These guidelines have not changed, but the number of schools has greatly increased; this has resulted in a serious crisis in teacher recruitment, aggravated by the fact that the excellent African schoolteachers of the colonial period have often moved up to high administrative or political positions and have been replaced by less qualified people. Just as in France, and for the same reasons, young people have preferred to prepare themselves for more prestigious careers or for better-paid jobs than teaching, while the social position of women has not generally risen sufficiently to allow for large-scale recruitment from the female population, which is what usually takes place in industrialized societies. The result (still as in France!) is a

13. This does not mean that they should not also teach Russian or German to some of their technicians or scientific researchers.

14. I am not sure of the status of English in Zanzibar, where the situation at the time of this writing is slightly anarchic.

15. Written in 1964. In 1965 three other states adopted national African languages: Rwanda (Kinyarwanda), Burundi (Kirundi), and the Central Africa Republic (Sango). Botswana and Lesotho have since adopted seTswana and seSotho, respectively. Tanganyika and Zanzibar have united under the name of Tanzania.

Schema of Sociolinguistic Division of a Modern African State

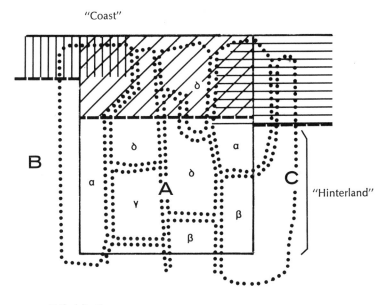

•••••••• Tribal limit

————— Political boundaries between country A and its neighbors, B and C

━━━━━ Break in communication with the outside world

Sociological zone of use of the "colonial" language

The cross-hatched zone represents the minority in country A which has a monopoly on the instrument of international communication.

The "coast" is a sociological rather than a geographical zone: it is the zone of maximum schooling and of maximum contact with the outside world. The tribes of this region are favored by their situation, particularly those (α) which inhabit a frontier position, which gives them access to two languages of wide communication. The tribes of the hinterland (β, δ) are less favored, especially those which, like γ, live in enclaves.

lowered quality of teaching, which creates serious problems at a time when the need for qualified personnel is so obvious.

This is only one aspect, and one of the better known, of the many contradictions which Africa constantly faces in its development. This particular case belongs to a more general problem, that of communication—meaning circulation of information—in today's Africa. The terms "French-speaking Africa" and "English-speaking Africa" tend to cover up the real nature of the problem. Obviously, it is important to wonder how Ghanaians speak to Guineans (or Senegalese to Zanzibaris, etc.), but it is far more important to know how Ghanaians speak to Ghanaians, and Guineans to Guineans. The answer to this last question is clearly "in English and in French, respectively"; but such an answer is only partially correct, since, as I have said, French and English are spoken by only a minority of the population.

Power, it is true, is in the hands of this minority. Herein lies one of the most remarkable sociological aspects of contemporary Africa: that the kind of class structure which seems to be emerging is based on linguistic factors. On the one hand is the majority of the population, often compartmentalized by linguistic borders which do not correspond to political frontiers; this majority uses only African tools of linguistic communication and must, consequently, irrespective of its actual participation in the economic sectors of the modern world, have recourse to the mediation of the minority to communicate with this modern world. This minority, although socially and ethnically as heterogeneous as the majority, is separated from the latter by that monopoly which gives it its class specificity: the use of a means of universal communication, French or English, whose acquisition represents truly a form of capital accumulation. But this is a very special kind of capital, since it is an instrument of communication and not one of production. It is nevertheless this instrument, and generally this instrument alone, which makes possible the organization of the entire modern sector of production and distribution of goods.

The personal advantages which members of the minority group can gain from this situation are less significant today than before independence (an interpreter is less essential at the level of local relations) but remain, nevertheless, considerable. The damage to the cohesion of the whole collectivity, however, has increased wherever the evolving class structure takes the form of a dichotomy between the privileged and the nonprivileged, which is usually the case. The roots of this problem did not change with the departure of the colonizers; the Africans who have taken the destiny of their countries into their own hands must, like the colonial administrators of yesteryear, resolve the problem of linguistic communication. The development they plan for their countries implies transformations in all areas of life, and these transformations are generally conceived and expressed in European terminology at the management level; but they must be passed on to the masses in easily comprehensible ways.

It is indeed difficult, even if one has a strong coercive system, to lead a revolutionary program of development successfully without the cooperation of those who must carry it out and who are eventually to benefit from it. According to the classical formula, one must "form them and inform them." Information will be much more effective if it passes directly from the speaker to the listener with a minimum of distortion or loss of power. Every translation constitutes a break in transmission and a loss of effectiveness, in some cases even becoming an insurmountable obstacle. Imagine, for example, psychoanalysis or psychotherapy with three actors: the sick person, the analyst, and the interpreter. The problem is very serious: at a time when the neuroses of acculturation are multiplying at a nerve-wracking pace, particularly in the towns, most psychiatrists (including African ones) have no direct access to the obsessions of their patients unless they understand their language. (As the studies done by Jean Rouch and Margaret Field seem to show, traditional African medicine does possess psychotherapeutic methods which are just as effective as European medicine, if not more so.)

Moving away from an ideological and more or less emotional level to a rigorously concrete and down-to-earth level, we arrive thus at the problem of the choice of national languages or, more precisely, official languages—languages of communication. The problem remains that of communicating the information necessary for the achievement of development programs with a maximum of effectiveness and economy. Three possible solutions exist: the use of a European language, previously taught to the group one wishes to reach; the direct formulation of the problems in vernacular languages; the use of translators and interpreters.

Large-scale teaching of French or English presupposes the resolution of the problem: it would require the kind of material and financial resources which would have been the result of spectacular prior economic development. I base this, obviously, on the hypothesis of the simple extension of the existing educational system, which is a continuation of the colonial one, which is itself in the best cases modeled on the European system. In this hypothesis it would also be necessary to wait at least a generation before reaching full efficiency. But time is of the essence.

One might thus be tempted to believe that the most efficient solution would be the use of local languages. This path really includes as many, if not more, pitfalls, except in certain particularly favorable cases. The principal factor here is the political factor, which is linked to the ethnic and linguistic heterogeneity. Whatever the true feelings of the population are toward the old colonial power, the language of the colonizers is, on the one hand, prestigious, being that of the modern ruling elite, and, on the other hand, it is emotionally neutral, since it belongs to no local tribe but rather can be common to peoples of different ethnic origins and may even have been the means by which members of tribes or castes who were previously subjugated emancipated themselves from their precolonial masters. Each local language is, moreover, intimately related to a tribal culture; thus use of a local language reinforces the attachment to a tribe, thereby going against the current of national sentiment, which is still only slightly developed. Use of *all* the local languages, should this be possible, would often lead to a fragmentation hardly conducive to nation-building. To impose certain of the local languages might provoke violent reactions by other linguistic groups; such circumstances led to a bloody uprising in Nigeria, when, shortly after independence, the Tiv of the Northern Region learned that Hausa was to be imposed on them.

The adoption of one or several local languages may, however, be a good solution in certain countries, under the following conditions:

(a) These countries must enjoy a certain degree of linguistic homogeneity, whether one means by this that only a few languages exist and have approximately equal political and demographic importance, or that the various languages in active use are closely enough related so that a common language can be created which will be acceptable to all (as is the case with written Yoruba or with standard Shona), or, finally, that one local language already plays the role of a lingua franca understood and accepted by the majority of the population (Swahili in Tanzania).

(b) The language chosen must have a transcription which is both precise and practical and, secondarily, which already possesses a certain corpus, written or recorded, which serves to encourage the learning of this language. If the only available newspapers, records, books, and so forth are all in French or English, one could scarcely expect the Bongo-Bongo to learn Wongo-Wongo.[16]

The situation of various states relative to their linguistic homogeneity varies considerably from one region to another. For geographic and ethnological reasons, the prize for the greatest heterogeneity doubtless goes to Cameroon and Nigeria. The greatest relative homogeneity is found in the Bantu zone, on the one hand, and in Western Sudan, on the other.

In general terms, the situation is the following:

A. Linguistically homogeneous states

1. Rwanda ⎫
2. Burundi ⎬ Kinyarwanda and Kirundi are spoken there.

16. Don't bother to look up these two groups on maps or in classifications. They ive on the outer limits of the Manganese Coast and southern New Poldevia.

3. Botswana: Tswana ⎫ These two languages are very close to each
4. Lesotho: Sotho ⎭ other.

Kinyarwanda and Kirundi can in fact be considered dialects of a single language. They are, furthermore, in Swahili's zone of extension, and this language serves as a common language for dealings with neighboring ethnic groups.

B. LINGUISTICALLY HETEROGENEOUS STATES, WITH ONE OR SEVERAL DOMINANT AFRICAN LANGUAGES

(a) *States with immediately usable languages*:

1. Nigeria: Western Region—Yoruba; Midwestern Region—Edo-Bini; Eastern Region—Ibo; Northern Region—Hausa. Remember that these languages are not in fact spoken by more than about half of the population and that their official use frequently meets with lively opposition, especially among the speakers of the following languages: Efik-Ibibio, Ijaw (East), Tiv, Kanuri, Fulfulde (North), languages which were used by the British colonial system in administration and education.

2. Zanzibar and ⎫ Swahili is and has been the language used.
3. Tanganyika[17] ⎭

4. Kenya: Swahili predominates in fact, but provokes unfavorable reactions, especially among the Kikuyu and Lwo.

5. Uganda: Ganda, the dominant language, meets with strong politically motivated opposition outside of Buganda; Swahili is widely used.

6. Malawi: Nyanja.

7. Rhodesia: Shona, a lingua franca created by the missionaries three decades ago, has an important role but is not dominant.

8. Zambia: Bemba seems to be the dominant language.

9. Swaziland (Ngwane): Swati.

(b) *States without immediately usable languages*:

1. Senegal ⎫ Sociological predominance of Wolof.
2. Gambia ⎭

3. Mali: the majority of the population uses forms of Mande, from which a generally intelligible common language could easily be built.

4. Upper Volta: predominance of More (Mossi), with politically motivated opposition.

17. Since April, 1964, federated into a single state: Tanzania.

5. Gabon: Fang actually predominates.
6. Comoro Islands: dialects of Swahili are spoken; Arabic is the language of religion and prestige.
7. Rio Muni: Fang.

C. States with moderate linguistic heterogeneity

(a) *Those with immediately usable languages*:

1. Ghana: predominance of the Kwa group, with several languages being well-documented: Ewe, Twi, Fanti.
2. Togo: predominance in the south of Ewe; but the lingua franca, Gɛ, or "Mina," differs markedly from standard Ewe.

(b) *Those with only untranscribed or badly transcribed languages*:

1. Niger: virtually evenly divided among Jerma-Songhaï, Hausa, Fulfulde, Kanuri, and Tamahiq.
2. Dahomey: predominance of Yoruba and Fɔ̃ in the south, of Berba and "Dendi" (commercial Jerma) in the north.
3. Guinea: more or less equally divided among Malinke (northern Mande), Susu (southern Mande), Pular (western dialect of Fulani), and, secondarily, Kpele and Kisi.

D. States with great linguistic heterogeneity

1. Sierra Leone: main languages belong to different groups: Krio (Africanized English), Kpele, Timne, Bulom-Sherbro, Mende, etc.
2. Liberia: Afro-American, Timne, Vai, Basa, Grebo, Kpele, etc.
3. Ivory Coast: divided among the Mande, West Atlantic, Kwa, and Voltaic groups. Lingua franca: "Anyi-Baule" (Kwa) and "Dyula" (Mande).
4. Cameroon: about one hundred languages for four million inhabitants! Lingua francas: Pidgin, in Douala and to the west, "Yaounde-Bulu" in the south, Gbaya in the east, Mbum in the center; Fulbe (bastardized Fulfulde) in the north.
5. Chad: mosaic of little-known languages. A pidginized Arabic called Turku serves as the lingua franca in the north.
6. Central African Republic: another mosaic. Lingua francas: Sango and Lingala.
7. Congo-Brazza: very fragmented Bantu languages. Lingua francas: Lingala and the trade dialects of Kikongo ("Fiote," "Monokotuba").
8. Congo-Kinshasa: numerous Bantu languages, except in the north-

east; the Belgians used four official lingua francas: Lingala, Kongo, Luba, and Swahili.

N.B. Little is known of the situation in the Portuguese colonies or in the former German colony of South West Africa. In South Africa, the Nguni group predominates in rural areas; in urban centers, the lingua franca is "Kitchen Kaffir." Many Africans or "Coloreds" born in the city speak only English or Afrikaans.

Given this situation, even in those states of groups A and B, listed above, where local languages have been satisfactorily transcribed, it nevertheless remains true that any generalized use of these languages often produces considerable technical difficulties. The extremely rapid evolution of the total over-all social context requires that these languages adapt much more rapidly than the normal linguistic evolution, insofar as it is possible to define a "normal rhythm." Even where "linguistic engineering" (an American term meaning the systematic and organized adaptation of a language by acclimatization of neologisms corresponding to new ideas) is practiced, the question of time still intervenes. It appears to be impossible to accelerate the natural process beyond certain limits. The attempt to exceed these limits entails the risk of wasting millions on the preparation of useless translations, especially useless because, in certain fields, those for whom these translations would be prepared would be more interested in directly acquiring a foreign language.

Fewer difficulties arise in the area of the natural sciences, where a form of linguistic symbolism of a second degree is generally used and whose characters are virtually international, generally built on pseudo-Greek or pseudo-Latin, which form the foundation of what one might call "Common International Scientific." In any case, this involves, at least on a certain level, an esoteric code accessible only to the initiated, usually without reference to their own language. (Frankly, I am personally unable to decipher any meaning from such phrases as "plasma," "π meson," or "quantum." When a physicist fires them at me point blank, I respond with "syntagm," "tone shift," "vocoid," and "archiphoneme.")

What is much more important and much more difficult is to implant in another language certain notions involved with very basic down-to-earth techniques. The acceptance of these—much more frequently used but unknown in the receiving environment—depends largely on the choice of an appropriate terminology. On a more abstract level—that of social relations—the communication of any ideology poses more complex problems. Christian missionaries had this experience in the past; politicians are experiencing it now. Let us compare, for example, the following text from Sekou Toure, *L'Expérience guinéenne et l'unité africaine* (Paris, 1959), pp. 282–83:

COMMUNIQUÉ DU BUREAU POLITIQUE DU P. D. G.

Le Bureau Politique du Parti Démocratique de Guinée, après un examen approfondi de la conjoncture politique en Afrique, consécutive au référendum, après avoir analysé les conclusions de la réunion du Bureau du Comité de Coordination du R. D. A., tenue à Paris les 7, 8, et 9 octobre 1958.

Estime que la décision du Bureau du Comité de Coordination de faire adhérer isolément territoire par territoire à la Communauté, consacre la balkanisation définitive des Fédérations et compromet gravement l'Unité africaine, dont toutes les sections R. D. A. ont fait la raison essentielle de leur approbation du projet de constitution.

Le P. D. G. est stupéfait des déclarations nettes du Président du R. D. A., définissant la Communauté, non comme un moyen d'émancipation des masses africaines dans le sens de la souveraineté et de l'indépendance, mais comme une construction intégrant de façon définitive les États africains morcelés dans la Communauté française.

Le P. D. G. affirme l'incompatibilité manifeste entre sa conception de la personnalité, de la dignité et des véritables aspirations de l'Afrique et son appartenance au R. D. A., dont le Président prône maintenant sans ambiguïté le maintien de l'Afrique dans la subordination, sacrifiant ainsi la personnalité africaine et renonçant à la clairvoyance de son Secrétaire général Sékou Touré, dont le sens politique a permis à la Guinée de faire son choix décisif, donnant à l'unité africaine son sens véritable et faisant des aspirations d'indépendance des masses africaines une réalité vivante.

Sur la plate-forme de l'indépendance nationale et de la pleine souveraineté de la Guinée, le P. D. G. proclame solennellement qu'il ne se considère plus comme une section du R. D. A. et qu'il est désormais l'allié naturel de toute section R. D. A. ou P. R. A. ou de toute autre organisation démocratique qui s'affirmera clairement dans la lutte effective pour l'Unité africaine, inséparable de la lutte pour l'indépendance nationale, en vue de l'objectif final qui demeure historiquement la formation des États-Unis d'Afrique Noire.

PARAPHRASE OF THE COUNTERTRANSLATION
(Italics Correspond to French Words in the Text)

Communiqué du Bureau Politique *du P. D. G.*

Ayant considéré la situation *politique* en Afrique après le *référendum* ainsi que les décisions de la réunion du *Bureau* du *Comité* de *coordination* du *R. D. A.* réuni à Paris les 7, 8, et 9 octobre 1958;

Le *Bureau politique* du parti autonomiste de Guinée estime que la résolution du *Bureau* du *Comité* de *coordination* comme quoi chaque pays doit adhérer isolément à la *Communauté* est une cause de grave division entre les partis, et s'oppose aussi à l'unité en Afrique des *sections* du *R. D. A.* qui sont d'accord pour établir des liens communs;

Les déclarations du *Président* du *R. D. A.* comme quoi la *Communauté* n'est pas un moyen d'acheminer les Africains vers le self-government et l'indépendance, mais qu'elle a pour objet d'enfermer, séparément, les peuples africains dans la *Communauté française* surprennent le *P. D. G.*;

Le *P. D. G.* déclare que sa conception de la personnalité, de l'honneur et des vrais problèmes de l'Afrique ne peut s'accorder avec sa présence au sein du *R. D. A.* dont le *Président* a clairement affirmé que l'Afrique restait terre de domination, trahissant ainsi sa nature, de même qu'il a repoussé l'expérience du *Secrétaire général* Sékou Touré, dont l'habileté politique a permis à la *Guinée* de choisir la bonne façon de révéler le vrai visage de l'unité africaine, répondant ainsi aux aspirations des Africains à la liberté;

Dans l'intérêt de l'indépendance du pays et de la véritable souveraineté de la *Guinée*, le *P. D. G.* déclare fermement qu'il a cessé d'être une *section* du *R. D. A.*, et se déclare désormais lié fraternellement avec toute section du *R. D. A.*, du *P. R. A.*, ou de tout parti quel qu'il soit qui s'affirmera dans le combat pour l'union de l'Afrique, inséparable du combat pour l'indépendance nationale, afin de répondre au grand désir d'union des peuples négro-africains.

ANNOUNCEMENT OF THE POLITICAL BUREAU OF THE PDG

The Political Bureau of the Democratic Party of Guinea after intensive examination of the political situation in Africa, following the referendum and after analysis of the conclusions made at the Bureau of the Committee for Coordination of the RDA, held in Paris, October 7, 8, 9, 1958,

Esteems that the decisions of the Bureau of the Committee of Coordination to make each isolated territory adhere individually to the community constitutes the definitive Balkanization of the Federations and gravely compromises African Unity, which all sections of the RDA have made the essential reason for their approval of the constitutional project.

The PDG is horrified by the outright declarations made by the President of the RDA wherein he defines the Community, not as a method of emancipating the African masses in terms of sovereignty and independence, but as a framework for integrating the African states individually within the French Community.

The PDG affirms the obvious incompatibility between its conception of the personality, the dignity, and the real aspirations of Africa and its membership in the RDA, whose President openly and clearly now favors keeping Africa in subordination, thereby sacrificing the African personality and renouncing the foresight of its General Secretary, Sekou Toure, whose political wisdom allowed Guinea to make its decisive choice, giving African unity its real meaning and making the hopes of the African masses for independence a living reality.

On a platform of National Independence and of the full sovereignty of Guinea, the PDG solemnly proclaims that it no longer considers itself a section of the RDA and that it is henceforth the natural ally of any section of the RDA or PRA or of any other democratic organization which will take its stand in the real fight for African Unity, inseparable from the struggle for national independence, in view of the final goal, which has always been the formation of the United States of Black Africa.

Compare this text with the retranslation into French from its translation into Basa, mother tongue of Ruben Um Nyobe, the famous Cameroonian nationalist leader of Marxist tendencies:[18]

PARAPHRASE OF THE COUNTERTRANSLATION

(The Words in Italics Are in French in the Text)

Announcement of the Political Bureau *of the PDG*

Having considered the *political* situation in Africa after the *referendum* as well as the decisions made at the meeting of the *Bureau* of the *Committee* of *Coordination* of the RDA meeting in Paris, October 7, 8, 9, 1958:

The *Political Bureau* of the autonomous party of Guinea esteems that the resolution of the *Bureau* of the *Committee* of *Coordination* by which each isolated country must adhere to the *Community* is a cause of grave division between the parties, and also opposes the unity within Africa of the *sections* of the *RDA* which have agreed to establish common bonds.

The declarations of the *President* of the *RDA* which indicate that the *Community* is not a means of leading the Africans to self-government and independence but that its object is to imprison the African peoples separately in the *French Community* surprise the *PDG*.

The *PDG* declares that the conception of the personality, the honor, and the real problems of Africa cannot be reconciled with its presence in the *RDA* whose *President* has openly avowed that Africa shall remain a dominated land, thus making himself a traitor to its nature, just as he repulsed the experience of the *Secretary-General* Sekou Toure, whose political ability allowed *Guinea* to choose wisely to reveal the true face of African unity, thereby responding to African hopes for freedom.

In the interest of the independence and true sovereignty of *Guinea*, the *PDG* declares resolutely that it has ceased to belong to the *RDA*, and

18. The Basa text and interlinear word-for-word translation can be found in my article "Sur les possibilités expressives des langues africaines en matière de terminologie politique," *L'Afrique et l'Asie*, no. 56 (Paris, 1961).

announces itself to be henceforth fraternally linked with any *section* of the *RDA, PRA*, or any other party which will take a stand in favor of the fight for African unity, inseparable from the fight for national independence, in order to respond to the great desire of the Black African peoples for union.

The difficulties involved in the second method suggested—the use of African languages—seem to be as significant as those involved in the first—the use of French or English. Thus we have recourse to a third method: the use of an interpreter. Governor Labouret (who was my predecessor at the "Langues O") once said: "There are four categories of interpreters: those who know French and the local language, those who know French but not the local language, those who know the local language but not French, and, the largest group, those who know neither language." The cynicism of this statement is partially justified. The interpreter should generally be considered a necessary evil—temporarily necessary, let us hope, but still necessary. What we need now is to replace the "filtering" interpreter of the colonial era with a "monitoring" interpreter. This amounts to saying that the technician must somehow learn how to convey the message to his audience in a language they readily understand. This presupposes that the interpreter has both linguistic and technical competence, thus, presumably, that he is a native son. Unfortunately, the least-developed areas are the least able to supply such people, precisely because of their backwardness. In addition, most technicians now receive a training which completely neglects this aspect of their function. The young specialists trained for radio and television provide the most outstanding example of this: they are trained to do everything except to communicate information to their countrymen who do not speak French.

Given the present situation in Africa, the most effective solution would seem to lie in a loose combination of the three methods, with emphasis varying according to local needs and desired results.

The teaching of European languages continues to fulfill a number of urgent needs. This does not mean that this instruction should remain exactly as it was during the colonial period. The methods used should vary with the goals sought. The French colonial educational system, based on the metropolitan model, may certainly pride itself on having produced a Senghor, a Camara Laye, or a Mongo Beti. One may nevertheless criticize it for not having taught hundreds of thousands of African peasant children who care nothing about Teilhard de Chardin how to read directions for using a tractor or a sack of fertilizer. The system of special elitist training reserved to the higher levels may have been defensible in a homogeneous society where middle-level groups formed themselves by self-propagation, if I may use the term. In Africa, this system has led to a great gap between the minister or executive, doctor or professor, and the millions of his illiterate underlings. I know African cities where it is easier to recruit an ambassador than a typist.

The solution to this problem doubtless lies partially in perfecting new teaching methods[19] which will give students a practical knowledge of French oriented to the local setting and to its needs, in such a way as to make the system most profitable.[20] Obviously, this means the end of papers on "The First Snows of Winter," but also, and more important- ly, it means adapting methods for teaching French to the local linguistic milieu. This has particular applications for the intensive campaigns for adult literacy, experiments in basic education, etc. The principle is very simple: before establishing the content and outline of lessons in French, one must find out the phonology and grammatical structure of the stu- dents' language and thus foresee probable difficulties and possible solutions. It was only in 1962 that the National Pedagogical Institute admitted the necessity for this; we are still awaiting (1964) the necessary means for putting it into practice. The same considerations apply also, of course, to the teaching of English.

Vernacular languages must occupy a privileged position in adult education (including literacy programs): it would appear difficult— although it has been tried, but without success—to ask peasants who return exhausted from their work to learn French *and* reading *and* writing *and* the use of fertilizers or advanced techniques of burnt- clearing—all this in several hours or several days. Methods such as Laubach's for teaching adult literacy classes require using the local language. More generally, if one wishes firmly to implant new techniques or new fashions of living, it is necessary to avoid creating in the minds of the students the impression that these things are foreign or extraneous, in a word, "white," and this rules out teaching through interpreters.

Furthermore, it is important that children should not be completely cut off from their milieu, and thus from their language, while receiving formal schooling in a European language. For this reason, milieu and language must enter the classroom together. Here I am thinking less of written books than of audio materials, whether tapes or records,[21]

19. Audiovisual methods are one possibility. I must nevertheless point out how useless it is to distribute tape recorders or television sets if there are no technicians capable of changing a fuse or fixing a loose wire.

20. The input/output ratio reaches barely 20 per cent for the primary schools in rural areas.

21. For some areas 78 r.p.m. records and record-players with hand cranks are an enormous advantage: the local blacksmith can repair these phonographs but not a battery-operated tape recorder.

which are less expensive to produce today than books with special type. This would probably be the surest and most economical way of guaranteeing the preservation and perpetuation of a whole oral literature, which now threatens to disappear rapidly, as the development of European-type education discourages its transmission by traditional methods.

The rules of classical composition now lead me to speak of the linguistic future of Africa. Since the experience of the past twenty years teaches us that any attempt at long-term predictions involving African problems are at best hazardous, I will limit myself to indicating the direction in which observable tendencies seem to be leading, without venturing to guarantee the validity of these extrapolations for any time period.

In the first place, it would seem that the diffusion and use of European languages, especially French and English, will increase, especially in those areas—which I call the "sociological coastline"—where the level of children enrolled in school has gone beyond the critical point. Presumably, we shall also witness an increasing interpenetration between the areas covered by these two languages: the demand for teachers of French in the former British colonies is growing appreciably, and vice versa. Moreover, the African states are profiting from the cultural competition which is growing between the French and the Anglo-Saxons. The Americans, in particular, are making considerable efforts to furnish teachers and audiovisual materials to any francophone African state which requests these.

We must also expect a rebirth of Arabic studies in Islamized countries. In the Western Sudan such studies have been losing ground since the collapse of the precolonial Muslim empires and also since the installation of European educational systems. I use the term "Arabic studies" rather than "Islamic studies" advisedly. Although the latter have also experienced a recent revival, the present tendency is to teach Arabic in secondary schools as a living language (often in place of Latin, a heritage of the colonial system) but not to associate it with Muslim theological or legal studies, which lie rather more within the jurisdiction of higher education.

Finally, due particularly to grants of numerous scholarships, German is regaining a role, and Russian is creating one. These roles, especially the Russian, will probably grow in importance but will not replace French and English, failing some unforeseeable upheaval.[22] Portuguese, on the other hand, may very well suffer a setback, although Brazil is striving somewhat to take up the banner of Lusitanian culture. Flemish has

22. Chinese still plays only a microscopic role, but. . . .

been swept away, and the unpopularity of Afrikaans would seem to leave few chances open to the various Netherlands dialects.

The very success enjoyed by French and English poses the problem of their local evolution. In the English-speaking areas we are doubtless witnessing the appearance of local dialectal variations which are often barely intelligible to a Briton or an American[23] who is not used to them. Some British academics have confessed to me that they can often understand the French spoken by a Senegalese or an Ivoirien better than the English of a Ghanaian or a Nigerian. To this the Nigerians or Ghanaians will reply, citing the Americans as an example, that they claim the right to have a special English, and willingly compare Tutuola with Senghor. The case of Sierra Leonean Krio leads one to think that, unless this evolution is controlled, it might lead to the formation of new languages with no international value, whose speakers would thus be obliged to learn . . . English. We have not yet reached this point. Several factors, such as the development of local universities and the increase of international contacts, should limit this evolution, but it remains quite likely that very marked variations from Received Standard English (as spoken, for instance, on the third program of the B.B.C.) will continue to be judged not only acceptable but even desirable.[24]

This form of nationalism, or rather of dialectal particularism, does not now exist among francophone Africans. The attitude expressed by the most nationalistic of these would be: "Since French is a foreign language in Africa, let us demonstrate our intellectual capacities by speaking it as well as possible." In this respect, it is significant that most French-speaking African governments have reacted with hostility to projects involving the use of "Elementary French"[25] in their schools, insisting rather on "the true French of France." We can, nevertheless, already observe some deterioration in the French taught in the schools, since, as I have already indicated, the promotion of many trained schoolteachers to high posts simultaneously with the increase in the number of primary schools has led to lowered standards of recruitment. French technical-assistance programs have made an effort to alleviate this situation, not only at the level of secondary and university education, where most of the professors are still French, but at the level where schoolteachers and their assistants are trained and where new methods

23. American English has some influence on these dialects through movies and some television programs.

24. Cf. the American example and also Broad Scots.

25. This early official terminology, really quite unwisely chosen, has since been replaced by the term "Basic French."

are being applied. These programs, however, remain largely experimental.[26]

Avoiding some dialectalization of the French spoken in Africa nevertheless seems difficult as Africa moves away from elite education to mass education and makes efforts completely to Africanize the leadership. The creation of dialects is not necessarily a bad thing, as long as mutual comprehensibility exists. One might envisage, moreover, the creation of two kinds of mutual comprehensibility: one between Africans of different ethnic groups, using a strongly Africanized dialect on the national or inter-African level, and the other international, serving the leadership, technicians, and others who must communicate with the outside world. I do not set forth such a situation as the ideal one but as a quite realistic possibility. Haiti, and to a lesser extent Canada, offer precedents of such situations. In general, it is probable that, at least at the higher of the two levels mentioned above, the dialectal divergences between the French spoken in Africa and in France will remain less marked than in the case of English.

In matters involving African languages, colonization provoked, and independence may accelerate, a tendency toward mixing, toward an increase of interferences, leading to the rather rapid unification of neighboring dialects and even of rather closely related languages. The great lingua francas, with intertribal extensions, should benefit from this situation at the expense of languages with little demographic importance or even of languages spoken by quite large numbers of people but not extending beyond the borders of one ethnic group. Some languages have already disappeared in the past several decades, disappearances which are as much to be regretted from the scientific viewpoint as those of the dodo or European bison. It would be desirable to proceed immediately to the collection of taped documents involving speech patterns threatened by a similar destiny in the near future, without, however, seeking to assure them an artificial survival but rather with a somewhat museum-like preservation in mind.

To return to the "major" languages: their extension corresponds to an increased need for communication which correlates with the rapid transformations taking place in Africa. This extension seems clearly to be accompanied by linguistic modifications which, in the cases I have studied, are tending toward a marked simplification of the morphology resulting (if we may be, as Kipling said, "bloody technical") in a diminution of redundance and an increase in the rapidity of transmission. In clear and practical terms, this translates as a simplification of

26. This work is going on in several centers, laboratories, and organizations: CREDIF, BEL, IPN, ENLOV (*that* is French!).

the grammar. For example, the following series of class agreements from standard Swahili,

1	*mtu*	m*dogo*	yu*le*	wa-*Ulaya*
3	*mti*	m*dogo*	u*le*	wa-*Ulaya*
5	*jambo*	ɸ*dogo*	li*le*	la-*Ulaya*
7	*kitabu*	ki*dogo*	ki*le*	cha-*Ulaya*
9	*kalamu*	n*dogo*	i*le*	ya-*Ulaya*, etc.

tends, in the most "pidginized" forms of the language, toward a unique simplified version,

$$\left.\begin{array}{l} mtu \\ mti \\ jambo \\ kitabu \\ kalamu \end{array}\right\} dogo\ yule\ ya\ Ulaya$$

with the same meaning ("this small person-tree-business-book-pencil of Europe"), but the syntactic relationships are now chiefly marked by the position of the various elements, the dependent nominals having taken an unchanging form and the extradependent prefix having ceded its place to the semiautonomous morpheme *ya*, which constitutes a real preposition.

As for the vocabulary, we observe the replacement of infrequently used words, corresponding to certain elements of the old context, by loanwords or neologisms corresponding to new ideas. In the same way, words with a high content of information—clear, very precise, corresponding to subtle nuances—give way to words with less information content but, because of this, more polyvalence. Thus, a language which distinguished between "hunger for meat," "famine," "hunger after work," "hunger-thirst for juicy fruits" will keep only one word, "hunger," which will take its precision from the context and by combining with other words. The elimination of three out of four words will allow many new words to enter the traditional stock (for example, "vaccine," "M.P.," "cinema").

Probably a good number of terms corresponding to these new ideas are borrowed from European languages, in ways analogous to cultural-linguistic borrowings into these languages ("alcohol," "algebra," "sputnik," "duenna," "macaroni"). Such loanwords often form an important part of urban African slang, frequently introduced by pidgin or trade dialects. Some of the most delightful will bear only a short life: a government minister in East Africa is a *mu-benzi* (from the name of the car preferred by the high government officials). A pompous, self-important man in Lagos is a *degol*, etc. It seems likely that those terms which will survive are more of the following nature: in Bulu, *wofis* (English "office"), *fulis* ("police"), *toyini* (German *tausend*, "thousand"); in Swahili, *meza* (Portuguese "table") or *shule* (German *Schule*, "school") or the many words the Islamized populations have borrowed from Arabic. African nationalists would be mistaken in taking offense at this, as long as these words are philologically and grammatically incorporated into the local languages, as in French *choucroute* (sauerkraut) and *boulingrin* (bowling green) as contrasted to the monsters in Franglais like the words *shoot*, *parking*, and *suspense* or Frenglish "voyeur," "attaché case," and "gourmet."

Factors which are completely alien to linguistics play a role in the spread or decline of some languages. First among these is the attitude of African governments, whether they confine themselves simply to choosing between the languages spoken in their jurisdiction with a view to using them on the radio, in school, or in the government, or whether, for political reasons, they strive to favor or bully certain ethnic groups by systematically encouraging the spread of a language or by forbidding its use.

Technical factors now play a large role in the diffusion of unwritten or rarely written languages. I am thinking not only of the use of certain languages to broadcast radio news, political instructions, education programs, and so forth, but also of the fact that certain types of recorded popular music belong specifically to one or another ethnic group. The popularity of Ghanaian or Nigerian "high life" has in this way contributed to the diffusion of some languages in the Kwa group, while the success of the cha-cha's and merengues in the Brazzaville style has popularized Lingala. Generally speaking, modern techniques for recording and broadcasting tend to favor oral forms of expression, and this can play a great role in the preservation and renewal of traditional African cultures. In this fashion, the folkloric broadcast of Radio-Libreville, "Knowledge of Gabon," devoted to poetry and traditional music, was widely heard in South Cameroon and in Congo-Brazzaville; certain of its musical themes—both words and tunes—were adopted far from their original source. Similarly, thanks to records certain Bambara or Malinke *griots* have found an audience with a common background, something they could not have had twenty years ago.

All of these electronic techniques have one thing in common: even if they sometimes cost less than books, they remain very expensive in terms of the minimal financial resources of most African nations. Those people from the African nations whose economy is relatively prosperous, whose budget allows the installation of powerful transmitters, and whose standard of living allows the rather large-scale sale of machines and records will thus see the greater diffusion of their languages compared with their poorer neighbors. This fact works to the advantage of linguistic concentration but might also provoke nationalist reactions: many countries, for admittedly nonlinguistic reasons, have already begun to regulate imports of records and radios with varying degrees of strictness.

Still within the field of politics, pan-African ideology plays an ambiguous role. Insofar as principles are concerned, many of its militants call themselves supporters of the exclusive use of various local languages; but, on the practical side, the self-interested opposition which such policies inspire often tends now to favor the simultaneous extension of French, English, and Arabic. At the other extreme, the anarchy which reigns in part of Central Africa is conducive to bringing about the setback of European languages without, however, in the short range, benefitting any African language as such: raids by armed bands, minor or massive exoduses, the carrying-off of women and children from villages where all the men have been massacred, will considerably complicate the linguistic geography of the Congo-Kinshasa. The reader will understand that such situations make the job of a prophet difficult.

CHAPTER V

The Spoken Word and the Written Word

"Honneur de l'homme, saint langage": major elements of the ethnography of words. Education, taboos, politeness, secret languages. Is there a literature of illiterates? A parenthetical note on writing: imported alphabets, African alphabets. Permanence as a literary criterion. Talking drums: a false mystery. Current problems in literary expression. Relationship between the choice of a language vehicle and the size of the audiences. Electronics forever. The bat and the census.

Language is expression—a personal expression at the individual level, obviously, but always within the more general framework of a culture or a civilization. In this sense, the most interesting study, although the most difficult to undertake, would be of the daily familiar, informal expression—of women at the market or at their laundry, of men in a meeting hut or under the palaver tree, of children playing games. Such speech has been barely touched on until now, but with widespread use of tape recorders such studies will no doubt increase, just as the recorder has already transformed the conditions for ethnolinguistic inquiries. Meanwhile, we must limit ourselves to broad outline sketches, which are necessarily and unfortunately quite vague.

To begin, we can, I suggest, set forth the principle that, throughout Black Africa, language—or rather, speaking, or speech—is taken very seriously, even at the level of trivial or daily affairs. My opinion, contrary to Durkheim's, is that so-called primitive societies do not polarize the profane and the sacred but rather the pure and the impure. This way, each word is sacred or sacral or may at least become so under certain conditions. In many societies the Word is the web linking the world, and careless usage of a word may upset this system and provoke grave problems. Putting it another way, a word is effective, either by itself or by association with certain rites. Also, such rites would reinforce the effectiveness of the word rather than confer effectiveness on it.

The organizing principle on which language-teaching has tradition-ally been carried on was no doubt based on this fundamental principle rather than on well-conceived ideas of inherent grammatical correct-ness: solecisms were corrected, not because they were displeasing, or confusing to the transmission of information, but because the attack they posed on the regularity of the language might have repercussions on the very order of the world, especially from the moment when the child, nearing puberty, lost his "neutral" character to become a trans-mitter of life, or, as is said in many languages, a "real person" (for example, Bulu *nyă-moto*). The essential thing, then, was to learn when to speak and when to remain silent: *Kusema kuzuri, kutosema kuzuri* ("To speak is good, not to speak is good"), according to a Swahili proverb, implying the importance of choosing the time and the place.

The next important step as the child became a sexual creature in-volved teaching him what could or could not be said, and to whom and when. Something of this attitude obviously remains in present-day Europe. At least in my generation one was brought up to believe that certain expressions were "unladylike," and even today one is still told: "Come, now! Not in front of the vicar!" In Africa such language rules retain a stronger social and magical significance, affecting not just the vocabulary and the ideas permitted or forbidden to certain age groups or sexes but also the delivery and pronunciation. Among certain ethnic groups, women pronounce certain phrases differently from the men, leading some observers to conclude, without sufficient study, that special feminine dialects exist.[1] Elsewhere the elders enjoy special pronuncia-tion privileges; sometimes the chiefs or notables must never raise their voices or, conversely, are the only ones permitted to do so.

Some prohibitions or taboos are by nature analogous to familiar European ones: for instance, rules of decency concerning the explicit names for excretory or reproductive functions and their organs, al-though these are not generalized; rules against speaking of evil things, such as the name of a dangerous animal (especially snakes) or of an unfortunate event (a sickness, accident, or death) which must not be mentioned for fear that it will come to pass. Other prohibitions have

1. I once knew an administrator who had learned the local language in bed and consequently never ceased to amuse the local population with his feminine locutions.

more specific application and are often referred to as *hlonipha*, from the name of a Zulu custom which forbade people under pain of death to pronounce the name of the reigning king or even any combination of syllables which might evoke his name in even the form of an accidental pun. If the *hlonipha* should be applied in France, we could not use such words as "Gauls," "goal," or "gall." In the Nguni group the *hlonipha* was permanent, which meant that terms corresponding to current ideas had to be borrowed from neighboring languages or even that the meaning of words had to be changed—as if we had to replace "Truman" with the French *vrai homme* or substitute "a real person" or "one who doesn't lie." In other societies this taboo applied only during the king's lifetime. Among many groups similar prohibitions still exist today concerning family relationships. Usually these refer only to the names of blood relatives or of relatives by marriage to whom a particular respect must be shown. The origin of *hlonipha* and of analogous family taboos seems to lie in the belief that by pronouncing someone's name one can exercise a magic power over him. For this reason many Africans have a secret name, which is their "real" name and is mentioned only to their most intimate friends. In the Cameroon I once had a cook, who, after four years of loyal service, came to me one evening when he was drunk and, to show me his confidence, told me his name and his son's—which later, when he became sober and nervous about his indiscretion, I assured him I had not understood.

The teaching of gestures is—or was—closely associated with the teaching of words. In Black Africa no system of intertribal silent language seems to exist comparable to that of the North American Plains Indians. What one often does find, in addition to forbidden gestures (such as the very widespread prohibition on showing a finger), are obligatory gestures which substitute for words or complete them. In southern Cameroon, for example, it would be unseemly to pronounce a number one wished to cite: one uses the interjection corresponding to the unspoken number, and the questioner himself pronounces the number.

This can be a simple process. To use a Bulu example:

mebilí bɔ́n hŋ [show the little finger, ring finger, and third finger]—*béláa.*
"I have children . . ."—"three."

Or it may be more complicated:

makómbo silí tɔyíní hŋ [little, ring]—*ebaé!*
"I want francs, of thousands . . ."—"two!"
á mintét hŋ [the five fingers in a fist]—*mítán!*

"And, of hundreds . . ."—"five!"
á awóm̀ hŋ [index finger]—*dá!*—*á hŋ*
"And, of tens . . ."—"one!" "and . . ."
[little finger, ring finger, left middle finger, and the five fingers of the right hand in a fist]
m̀wɔm!
"eight!"

"[I want 2518 francs."]

Obviously this is precise and without possibility of misunderstanding.

While discussing figures, I might mention that, in addition to the "manually" based systems, whether 5 (1, 2, 3, 4, 5, 5 + 1, 5 + 2, . . . 2 × 5, 2 × 5 + 1, 2 × 5 + 2 . . .) or 10 (1, 2, 3, 4, 5, 6, 7, 8, 9, 10, 10 + 1, 10 + 2, . . .), which are the most widespread, there are also base-20 systems, for instance among the Yoruba; and, more or less everywhere, but especially in West Africa, one finds traces of a base-8 system. This latter system possesses a magical value and serves as the basis for an occult science or cabalistic ritual, for which certain authors have postulated an Oriental origin. Such a conclusion seems far-fetched, for this base-8 system is quite shrouded in uncertainty, as is the case with almost all that involves magic, even the special use of language.

The term "magic" perhaps does not apply here, and it would be much better to speak of rites and of ritual languages. Such a language may be no more than a formalized mode of current language: the use of special words, the prohibition of certain current words, the use of other current words but with a specific meaning, special prosody, and archaic forms whose meaning has often disappeared. It may also be a secret language, for which in theory only the initiated have the key. I say "in theory," for in addition to truly secret languages there are some which are in reality understood by the noninitiated, who must, however, pretend not to understand. A "secret" language thus plays a role analogous to that of some ritual masks, whose wearers remain depersonalized, with their identity erased behind the identity of the mask for the duration of the ceremony. In other instances the secret language is actually incomprehensible to the common people. Several kinds of these languages exist. In the first place, it may be a language foreign to the tribe involved, such as that of a relatively distant group from whom the rite may have been borrowed. A closely related example involves the use of a very archaic form of the local language or, at other times, of a language quite recently abandoned when a lingua franca or the language of a conquering people has been adopted. It is also possible to give a special meaning to ordinary words, as the Freemasons do (cf. F∴M∴ *canon* ["cannon"] = "glass of wine," which has passed into daily French usage), often by playing on related sounds. Another process belongs to slang forms like pig Latin (e.g., "Ig-pay atin-Lay") or Spoonerisms. In modern Africa secret languages of these kinds tend to play more of a social than a magical or ritualistic role. They are tending increasingly to become the codes of more or less marginal groups, such as schoolchildren, delinquents, truck-drivers, etc.

In other cases, also common today, only the ritual role subsists: there is no longer a true language; rather, the sounds produced are more or less accidental mixtures, generally dependent on fantasy or on the individual inspiration of those who produce them and which transmit no coherent information. Such is the glossolalia of syncretistic or pentecostal cults in West or Equatorial Africa. The "possessed" person is supposed to be speaking "English" or "Arabic" (Ivory Coast), "Latin" (Ivory Coast, Gabon, Congo), or even Russian or Chinese (Congo); the sounds he produces are "translated" or rather interpreted by the priest or cult master.

Let us return to ordinary language. I think one may contend that in societies which have not undergone too violent a cultural shock from the colonial impact, ordinary language is quite sophisticated, from the level of daily communication up. Verbal images and metaphors are frequently very abundant and combine with numerous references to proverbs and allusive aphorisms, difficult for a foreigner to follow; these, and the frequency of sonorous images and of the impressives and ideophones which characterize the languages of Africa, all help to create a kind of art out of well-conducted conversation. Enjoyable speakers often have a reputation extending beyond the limits of their villages. Orators too have a special place in various societies: on the one hand, the term we translate as "chief" may really mean "he who speaks to the people" or "he who speaks for the people" (Fang: *ǹdzóó bur*). Elsewhere one finds a "chief's mouthpiece," a royal orator at the chief's court, who is a true minister of words and whose political role may be considerable, so much so that certain explorers sometimes confused such officials with the real chief.

Oratorical art thus marks a sort of bridge between ordinary language and oral literature, the latter being characterized, it seems to me, by a certain permanence in time and space, closely bound to its highly developed formalization.

Here it becomes necessary to open a long parenthesis concerning the very expression "oral literature," a term denied by some on etymological grounds: no literature without *litterae*, letters or writing; Africa, a land without writing, could have nothing more than folklore. The annoying part of this argument is that Africa *has* writings which have been useful for producing literary works. And even if it had not, the term "folklore," insofar as it has become somewhat pejorative, could not do justice to the richness and beauty of these productions of the verbal art which many of us persist in calling "oral literature." But, let us look first at writings.

The transcriptions presented in various parts of this book are sufficient indication that Latin characters, modified as need be, are very widely used as graphic methods for the preservation of African texts. But while the first attempts date from the seventeenth century, there are much more ancient precedents. Without mentioning the possible penetration of Egyptian hieroglyphics, which remains to be proven, the Libyco-Berber *tifinagh* alphabet still used by the Tuareg must have crossed the Sahara three or four centuries before Christ. Its success, however, has been much less notable than that of Arabic, which was probably introduced toward the eight or ninth century of our era and is attested with certitude by the eleventh-century inscriptions at Gao.

Since this work is devoted to African languages, I can do no more than mention the existence of a rather abundant historical, theological, and judicial literature written in Arabic by the literate black scholars of the Western Sudan and the East Coast. Only part of this has been translated into various European languages. I must, on the other hand, stress the fact that the Arabic alphabet, adapted to the phonetic system of the users by the device of supplementary diacritical marks,[2] has been used to write texts in Hausa, Swahili, Fulfulde, Kanuri, Nupe, Songhaï, and Mande—that is, in the languages of peoples Islamized at rather early dates. As far as we know, the first four of these languages have the most extensive literatures of this kind. In fact, only a very small fraction of these literatures has come down to us: numerous manuscripts were destroyed, either during wars or during the troublesome periods accompanying the rise and fall of the great Sudanic empires or the struggle against the Portuguese in the Indian Ocean or at the moment of colonial conquest. Other manuscripts have been preserved, but their owners today are seldom willing to show them to foreigners, particularly Europeans. Still others gather dust in the libraries and archives of Europe under the heading of "illegible Arabic manuscripts" —obviously, for they are not in Arabic! Some efforts to recover and photograph all documents of this kind have recently been launched under the sponsorship of several African universities, and the first results are very promising. Unfortunately, these efforts came a bit late,

2. Such alphabets are generally known as *ajami* from an Arabic word meaning "indigenous."

for much more practical Latin transcriptions are increasingly substituting for the *ajami*;[3] thus the Fulani, Swahili, and Hausa interest in preserving manuscripts written with Arabic characters has greatly diminished.

What we know of these manuscripts attests to a definite originality, even though many of their authors sought to follow systematically the models suggested by Arabic literature. A marked difference separates them from the oral literature of the same population. This results from the fact that written literature, even in the vernacular languages, aimed only at a rather limited elite group and, what is more relevant, was not bound by the same formalized constraints as oral literature.

The Arabic alphabet, even in the form of *ajami*, is as much of an importation as the Latin one. In addition to these alien systems of writing, one finds several of African invention which seem to be of quite recent origin: Mom ("Bamoun") in the Cameroon, Vai, Basa, Mende, and Kpele in Sierra Leone and Liberia, Nsibidi among the Efik of Eastern Nigeria. The Bamoun script is the best known. This script has the special attribute of having run through virtually the entire evolutionary cycle of graphic systems during the life of its inventor, the *fon*, or sultan, of Foumban, Njoya the Great (c. 1880–1933). Indeed it was at the end of the past century that Njoya proclaimed that "the Muslims and Christians have their writing. The Bamoun must have theirs." He then composed, and imposed, an initial system of 350 hieroglyphics, each of which represented the notion to which it corresponded in a quite realistic fashion. After several years, the designs were simplified: they passed to the stage of ideograms—nonrealistic symbols, each corresponding to a notion. In 1911 came an important new advance: the ideograms took on a phonetic value; their number was reduced to 80, with each representing a syllable. Ultimately, in 1918, a final improvement allowed the Bamoun script to pass to the alphabetical stage, wherein each sign corresponds to a phoneme.

In this way, the Bamoun proceeded from a first stage, wherein the pictorial hieroglyphic representing a personality seated on a throne (♗) meant "king," to a second stage, wherein the design was simplified (♗) but kept the same meaning of "king," then to (♱), symbol of the syllable (*fõ*), derived from the word *mfõ* ("king"), and finally to (♱),

3. Arabic script, for instance, has characters for only three vowels, whereas the languages to be transcribed have a minimum of five; there exists no character corresponding to such phonemes as /p/, /v/, etc. The conventions adopted by various scribes to bridge these gaps were not the same, and certain texts are very difficult to read, even for those who know perfectly well both classical Arabic and their own language.

symbol of the phoneme /f/. In the same way, they went from (☒), a drawing of a fruit tree, meaning "to gather"—in Mom, *ri*—to the ideo- gram (☒), then to the syllabic sign (☒), [*ri*], and to the letter (☒), /r/; again, from the pot on a fire (☒), meaning "to cook" [*na*], to (ⴅ), "to cook," (ⴖ), [*na*], and ☒, /n/.

The Vai alphabet, also quite well known, is a syllabic alphabet which seems to have been the source of inspiration for other African alphabets in Sierra Leone and Nigeria. It was invented around 1830 by one Momolu Duwalu Bukele, who claimed to have received a revelation in a dream. Apparently all that Momalu did—but it is a great deal—was to transform a pre-existing system of ideograms or picto- grams into a syllabic system.[4] The Nsibidi writing of the Efik seems to be in a transition phase, its characters sometimes representing a complex notion and sometimes a sound. This writing is not well known, since it belongs to an initiation group which uses it both to enable its members to communicate among themselves and to fashion amulets and magic charms. In Yoruba, Ewe, and Fon territories, from Nigeria to Togo, it seems that the geomantic signs of the *fa* or *ifa* divination cult also constitute a system of proto-writing which is the exclusive prerogative of the initiates. Similar phenomena have been observed in the Sudanic zone, among the Bambara. I myself discovered that the signs engraved on the pieces of the Cameroonian game of *abia*, a form of tarot which serves simultaneously as a game of chance and as a divination system, corresponded also to a system of initiatory proto-writing which is lost today. From all this, it would seem extremely probable that all of Black Africa was much more initiated into writing systems than the first observers thought. I use the word "initiated" deliberately, for it is precisely the initiatory character of these graphic systems which allowed them to pass unperceived.

Closing the parenthesis opened about writing, I return to that charac- ter of temporal and geographic permanence that I designated above as the principal criterion of oral literature. One can, clearly, also regard elaborate form as the principal criterion permitting us to speak of literature in terms of the formula *literary:nonliterary::elaborate: nonelaborate*. I personally reject this approach, partly because, as I have already pointed out, even everyday communication is often marked by a high degree of elaboration, partly because certain genres, subjected to very rigid formal constraints, like political or forensic speeches,

---

4. The difference between ideogram and pictogram is that the former does not seek, or no longer seeks, to give a realistic representation of the object it symbolizes.

produce no durable works but "bits and pieces" with a *hic et nunc* usefulness, an immediate function. These are not preserved in the collective patrimony of a social group, in its cultural memory, while certain works, sometimes subjected to rather less rigorous formal restraints, are preserved. I would thus propose the formula: *literary*: *nonliterary*::*perennial*:*nonperennial*, with formalization or elaboration no longer intervening except as methods of assuring perennialness.

I should point out that, until the invention of the phonograph, any oral literature was subjected to much more stringent formal restraints than a written literature. Paper holds everything, and a graphic form suffices to ensure the preservation of a literary work through time or its diffusion in space, no matter what form the work takes or whether or not it has received a favorable public reception. Stendhal was able, as he took pride in saying, to write in 1835 for the public of 1885; my friend the *mbomo mvêt* Ela Obam of Ebolowa (Cameroon) would not know how to compose for an unborn audience, nor could he adopt an unusual poetic form which might prevent his contemporaries from keeping and passing on his works. In the same way, at the Bastille, the Marquis de Sade could cover reams of paper without much thinking of any public, but an illiterate author put into solitary confinement would see his works lost as soon as they were pronounced. In other words, it is impossible to create an oral literature without an audience; or, more precisely, in the absence of such an audience, such a creation is as though nonexistent.

It is very appropriate to bring music into our discussion because restraints upon the form of African oral literature most frequently involve the tonal and melodic structures of these languages—which we are beginning to know—and their rhythmic structures—about which we are almost totally ignorant. In Africa, literature is virtually inseparable from music. Works on a large scale, if they are not generally sung, are most often chanted (or recited in a singsong manner); they are almost always accompanied by musical instruments and are interspersed with sung sections. Let us note in passing that the distinction between prose and verse is very difficult and much debated.[5] In many cases, the best one can do is to paraphrase Monsieur Jourdain's philosophy teacher (who, like his student, practiced linguistics without realizing it)[6] by setting up an opposition *prose*:*nonprose*, while waiting for African linguists to untangle and define the metrical

5. Except, obviously, where this distinction results from Arabic models (Islamized regions: Fulani, Swahili, Hausa, etc.) or, more recently, from European ones.

6. Or perhaps realizing it: the ridicule of Molière and later Voltaire caused a century-long delay in France in the field of linguistics.

rules of their languages, a problem on which several are currently working.

An analysis of the content of different African literary genres does not fall within the limits of this book, yet these genres are as numerous and varied as ours. I will content myself with pointing out that, as one would expect in civilizations which take words very seriously, this literature almost never has a gratuitous character ("art for art's sake"), nor is it generally the expression of egotistic feelings or individual egotistical aesthetics. This does not mean that personal creativity and talent have no part: many works are in no way anonymous but, quite to the contrary, begin with a kind of genealogy extending from the current interpreter to the original author. But such individual creativity operates in the very strict framework of expression of a culture and of a social structure. This implies a very committed literature, often with a very openly didactic character. Even the most distracting and amusing works[7] often have an esoteric background, comprehensible only to the initiated, and thus a social function surpassing their basic pleasure value.

Professionals, "men of words"—like our "men of letters"—are often segregated, cut off in a social group, whether they form, like the Sudanic *griots*, a caste both scorned and privileged, or whether they belong, on the opposite extreme, like the Tutsi genealogist-poets of Rwanda and Burundi or the *bebomo mvêt* and *beyía biá* of Cameroon and Gabon, to a virtually sacerdotal class, highly honored, with difficult and restricted entry. The essential function of all is both ritual and political. Even the amateurs, the nonprofessional storytellers, must conform to very strict rules: there are masculine stories and feminine ones, works recited in the day and others at night, which can only be told after sundown, others which belong to certain families or which are not used except in certain circumstances or at certain times, etc.

Riddles, proverbs, slogans, and songs of praise make up the four categories found almost universally. These have considerable social importance and generally a very specific linguistic structure. They frequently form a system of cross-references, symbolizing and perpetuating certain kinds of social relations. In West Africa, a trial or a political discussion often takes the form of a barrage of proverbs, slogans, and allusions to riddles or to praise names, totally incomprehensible to outsiders, particularly since two or three levels of meaning may be superimposed, one on another.

7. For example, the fables with animal themes, from which the fables of La Fontaine may well have stemmed, via the *Roman de Renart* (Reynard the Fox) and *Aesop's Fables* (Aesop = *Aethiops*, Greek for "the Black, the African," according to the late Professor Alice Werner of London).

Linguistically, this entails short sentences, with a rhythm and characteristic tonal contour which are well-suited to transmission by drums.

Drummed languages and the closely allied whistled or shouted languages interest linguists and musicologists alike, as well as, alas, film-makers and cheap novelists. The latter have given only too much credit to the myth of the pan-African "bush telegraph" or "African telephone," sending news from Dakar to the Cape of Good Hope in the blink of an eye, while brave explorers "leave the bush for the savanna" (I really heard this in the soundtrack of an "educational" film) and go forth on safari bristling with rifles "to the haunting rhythm of the drums" (oh, lovely hostesses and distinguished guests). I have myself in fact frequently observed the astounding rapidity with which certain news is diffused in Africa. Thus, six weeks after the outbreak of the Mau Mau revolt, my children brought back from their Togolese school—more than 3,500 kilometers from Kenya and in a completely different ethnic and linguistic environment—the famous war cry *mayibue*, whose meaning remains quite unclear to this day (it does *not* mean "Come back, Africa"). The astonishing aspect of this affair is not that this detail traveled 3,500 kilometers in six weeks but that it did it by word of mouth, since neither the newspapers nor the radio had mentioned it. In no way was this a question of the "mysterious talking drums," understood by no European except Tarzan and District Commissioner Sanders of the River.[8]

The principle of drum transmission is actually quite simple. The drummer reproduces on his instrument the rhythms and tones characteristic of the sentence he wants to transmit. The choice of expression is thus not entirely free, since what one might call "the tune" must not contribute to confusion. Recourse is most generally had, therefore, to more or less stereotyped periphrases. In the Bulu system in Cameroon, for example, the "tune" of the word *ngóvíná*, "administrator, prefect" (low-high-high-high) is identical to that of other loanwords, such as *ṅkáfíntá*, "carpenter." In its place, then, they substitute the expression *ŋwéé | bòt èlàŋ*, "he who kills people unnecessarily" (low-high long—short pause—low-low-low), which permits no confusion! In the same way, *bíngá*, "women" (high-high) does not have sufficiently structured individual identity to be transmitted without confusion: new words are sent—*àyɔ̀ŋ | tɛ̀ | ṁféndék*, "tribe without penis" (low-low long—short pause—low—short pause—low-high-high), etc. The drum used, the *ṅkúl*, is a cylinder of wood, hollowed out along one of its sides; the

8. Perhaps Alan Quatermain also. The saving grace of Edgar Rice Burroughs, Edgar Wallace, and Rider Haggard is that they inspired several authentic Africanist careers.

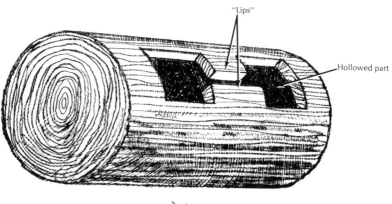

Ǹkúl

two walls or "lips," since they are of unequal thicknesses, produce a
high tone (female) and a low tone (male), respectively, the nuances of
length being dependent on whether or not one muffles the vibration of
the "lip" being struck. (See diagram.) The fabrication of these drums, to
which is linked a whole cosmic symbolism founded on the opposition
and the union of the sexes, used to be surrounded by great ceremony,
including a bloody sacrifice destined to "give force" to the instrument.
Nowadays the last of the drum-makers put advertisements in the local
paper in order to sell their product.

In the group of tribes living between the Sanaga (Cameroon) and the
Ogooué (Gabon) all communications on the talking drum begin with
the call signal of the person or the group being called, followed by the
call signal of the sender; then comes the body of the message, and finally
a cluster indicating the end of the transmission. The call signals in
question, *ndán*, often called "drum names," are really collective slogans
(*ndán* of the clan, the lineage, or the village), or individual ones, which
echo a past event, a great fact about an ancestor, a proverb, or a nickname.

Every man (women do not have the right to touch an *ǹkúl*) at the
moment of his initiation into manhood receives such a motto, drawn
from the hereditary patrimony of his lineage. It might happen, after a
glorious or ridiculous exploit, that a new motto would be devised and
added to the clan's stock. Here is one example of a message, borrowed
from the Bulu novel *Nnanga kôn* (*The Phantom Albino*), by J. L. Njemba
Medu:

1. *bìtá   bíbólè* │ *tè m̀fàŋ zèŋ*
   .   . .   .   °   ║ Indicates the person
   .   °   . . . .   ║ called (twice).
   war is-broken │ no good path ║
   "The war is lost; everyone for himself."

2. *támɛ́   zù* │ *àvól   àvól   àvó*
   . .   .   .   .   ║ Message (twice).
        °   ° ║
   please to come, │ quickly, quickly, quickly. ║
   "Come quickly, please."

3. *zíŋ   jàkɛ̀   ŋgbʷà   jàkɛ̀*
   .   ║ "Signature" of the
      . °   .   . °   ║ sender (twice)
   hatred goes away friendship goes away ║
   "Everything passes, everything breaks apart."

   ǹdòngò   óbàm   ndómán   óbàm   ńdòngò   àlɔ́ènɔ̀ w̌ɔ
   . . . . ° ║
   Ndongo of Obam   son   of Obam of Ndongo calls you ║
   "Ndongo Obam, son of Obam Ndongo, calls you."

2B *òm̀fété* │ *támɛ́   zù àvól   àvól   àvó*
   . . .   .   ° ║ Repetition of the
      .   . .   .   .   ║ message (twice).
   answer then │ come quickly quick quick quick ║
   "Answer! Please come quickly!"

4. *kèŋ   kèŋ   kèŋ   kèŋ   kèŋ*
   .   .   .   .   .   ║ Closing cluster.
   boom boom boom boom boom ║
   "Stop; end of broadcast."

(The black dots mark the clipped beats, the white circles the vibrated beats.)

Here the *ndán* of the person called is a historical allusion, while the sender's sign is a proverb. Following is an example of a *ndán* nickname which has become a lineage property:

àsà²à bíngá │ *tè   vɛ́   ǹsùbá*
   . .   .   °   ║
. . .   ║
he f . . . women │ without paying "bridewealth." ║

"He enjoys himself without paying for it."
(I prefer not to be more specific on the personality involved.)

The ability to play the *ǹkúl* lies not only in a sense of rhythm and timing or in the strength and suppleness of the wrists; equally essential is a perfect knowledge of the language, not only to enable one to tie the known periphrases together but also to invent others which will be immediately understood by the listeners. The *ǹkúl* is not only a machine for communicating over distances;[9] it is also a musical instrument, used to accompany certain dances. In the *ozíla*, for instance, a Bulu dance which enjoyed great success when the Cameroonian Ballet performed at the Théâtre des Nations in 1963, the *ǹkúl* "speaks" to the dancers, dictating various steps and changes to them by beating a counterrhythm to the rest of the orchestra and choir. This is an art form as complete as it is complex.

Farther west, in the Guinea forest and Sudanic regions, the all-wood talking drum is replaced by a pair of vertical drums, cylindrical or conical-cylindrical, with elongated shapes and a skin membrane stretched with wooden wedges. Here, too, the deep-voiced drum is "male," the high-pitched "female." This instrument is much more versatile than the wooden drum, since for each drum the musician has a choice between striking the center or the periphery of the skin, or even the wood, and he can allow the skin to vibrate for a long or short period of time. The versatility allows one to render faithfully such languages as Yoruba, which combines the three level basic tones (low, high, middle) with a series of complex tones (low-high, low-middle, middle-high, middle-low, high-low). Talking drums are one of the insignia of royalty; some royal drums were covered with human skin.

One last type is represented by the armpit drum, *gon-gon*, shaped like an hourglass, where differences of pitch and duration are accomplished by pressure from the elbow on the tension strings.

Whistled languages and bells with two pitches obey the same rules as shouted languages. These latter consist of modulated cries on one or two meaningless syllables or even on a single vowel, which carry much farther than ordinary spoken language. An analogous system seems to have existed until recently among certain European shepherds, as the "Tyrolean" or yodel of the Alps witnesses. Evidently a system of this kind functions much less well in a nontonal language, although it is not impossible elsewhere: it is easy, for example, to whistle certain fables of La Fontaine in a recognizable fashion, "The Raven and the Fox" doubtless being the best example.

The survival, and *a fortiori* the renewal, of African oral literature currently poses several grave problems. It would be eminently regrettable

9. The large *minkul*, almost a meter in maximum diameter, carry as far as 8 or 10 kilometers on a clear day without wind, if they are placed on top of an isolated hill.

to permit the loss of such an important part of humanity's cultural capital, for not only Africa would be impoverished by such a loss. Unfortunately this is what is happening. Several factors are responsible. In the first place, African languages are changing rapidly in all those regions where European influence has been extensive, especially because of general changes provoked in the social context and specifically because of the collapse of traditional education due to the competition of modern schools. Some oral literature, even certain works dating from only one generation ago, are no longer very well understood by the young, because the language used is obsolete. The second reason has a similar cause: certain texts are no longer learned, either because they were formerly taught in initiation schools which have now disappeared or because modern economic circumstances have dried up the recruitment of specialists. Thus, in Sudanic countries, the children of *griots*, even though they may not escape from their caste, can nevertheless, thanks to modern education, acquire an economic independence which frees them from following their father's profession, the most gifted being the first to leave. In Southern Cameroon the traditional prestige accorded a man of words has largely passed to the man of letters; the terms "writer" and "clerk" are still used to designate civil servants. Also, the new modern economic conditions are not conducive to teaching the great epics, whose recitation takes hours. In the past, in order to be allowed to learn one, a person had to begin by giving a daughter or a sister in marriage to the epic's "owner" (*mié-jiá*, "master of the song") and, in addition, take care of his needs and those of his entourage during the apprenticeship, which might last several weeks or months. On the present scale of "bridewealth," in 1964 this would represent an investment of several thousand francs (and I haven't even mentioned the necessity of obtaining the girl's consent!). Now a professional *mbomo mvêt* must have several such epics in his repertory. Although the profession is profitable, those who have capital to spend prefer to place it elsewhere.[10]

In addition to all artistic or cultural considerations, this decline in oral literature has already had consequences for economic development. As nothing, or almost nothing, has come to take its place, people are bored in the villages, and the young people leave the villages to join the unemployed in the cities, where amusements are less rare. This

10. Other reasons do exist, particularly the fact that the social prestige of these minstrels was closely tied to the system of rites and initiations, which has been almost totally destroyed by the arrival of Christianity. Because of this, among other reasons, a fear of what people will say has turned some minstrels' sons against their father's profession.

exodus in no way eases the job of agronomists or of urban police forces.

I present this argument since nowadays only economics is taken seriously. Being hardly an economist myself, I attach far more importance to the fact that, as I sometimes fear, Africa is in the midst of losing its soul. Negritude was doing rather well until lately, at least along the Seine, on both the Right Bank and the Left, and in intellectual discussions. Meanwhile, students in African bush schools were learning the "Tortoise and the Hare" by La Fontaine while forgetting local versions of the same theme. People in Paris and Rome were thus "saving" an African culture which was fading away in Nkoletotol (Cameroon) or Djerekpanga (Togo). After all, the French continue to glorify (in a language descended from Latin) Gallic ancestors of whom they know almost nothing. Africa will perhaps be spared a similar fate, thanks to the tape recorder.

One may well ask whether African literary expression should not commit itself to two fields of action: a written one, basically aimed at expressing Africa to the outsider, and an oral one, destined to perpetuate and to renew traditional expression within Africa itself. If the culture is to remain alive (i.e., evolving), these two sectors should continually interact and inspire each other.

We must indeed remember that one of the main problems currently posed for the African who has something to say, who wants to express himself on a literary plane, is that of an audience. Supposing that his mother tongue may be written down, or even that he might use one of the widespread African lingua francas, he can count on a maximum potential public of some tens of thousands of readers, a public which is, furthermore, geographically localized in a rather limited area. Besides, there is little chance that translation will enlarge the field of possible diffusion of his work; of all the abundant literature written by South African Bantu, only one work, the historical novel *Chaka*, by the Sotho Thomas Mofolo, has been translated into French, English, German, and Dutch—but the last three in fact are simply translations of the original translation by V. Ellenberger. On the other hand, the works in English by Peter Abraham or Ezekiel Mphalele and many others have, since their publication, enjoyed an international renown, which explains quite well the sudden concern of the South African government to "save Bantu culture," that is, to prevent the Bantu from making their voices heard in the world.

In choosing English or French in which to express himself, or rather to express his version of Africa and its problems, the African author automatically has access to a potential market ten times more important than that given to a work in Swahili or Hausa; above all, it is a market at once pan-African and universal, especially in view of the fact that the use of a European language greatly simplifies the problems of translation: in Germany or Italy there are far more people who know English or French than Yoruba or Xhosa.

The immediate profit gained by enlarging the foreign audience is offset by the fact that the author cuts himself off from a significant section of his local audience. What will frequently happen is that most of the people to whom the author addresses himself—and in whose name he speaks—will be incapable of reading him.

This rupture between the writer and what one would consider his natural audience surely affects his inspiration; a kind of current crisis in French African literature may be partially explained by this fact. At the same time, at the level of the community there exists another and more dangerous effect: the creation in Africa of a class literature, in a much more entrenched way than in Europe, insofar as a division may open up, not between the "cultivated" and "uncultivated" audience, but between two audiences with totally different cultural backgrounds— one literate, using European languages, and the other oral, using African languages. As I have said above, oral literature cannot exist without an audience. In the traditional setting, such participation is active, and listeners exchange traditional responses with the speaker, serving as a chorus for musical passages, loudly applauding the heroes and condemning the villains. Evidence indicates that this active participation becomes very difficult if the oral work is presented by mechanical means, although the audience may remain a collectivity—as is not the case for the printed medium. Similarly, sound reproduction allows the full use of musical accompaniment, which forms a basic part of certain genres, while the written form can only mutilate a work and give only an incomplete version of it.

The most hopeful and the newest factor introduced by the tape recorder is that, as with the printed works but in a much more complete and relaxed fashion, one can preserve and disseminate the literary work to a degree which was previously impossible. The audience for a talented *griot*, an imaginative minstrel, or a competent reciter of any traditional piece may in the future be as large as, or even larger than, the writer's audience. Fortunately this comes at a time when Africa still has some chance of escaping rock and roll or Liberace. African governments now have the technical means not only for saving traditional oral culture but even for renewing it.

I cannot resist the temptation to offer the reader as a gift at the end of this chapter an example of the modern adaptation, both social and linguistic, of a traditional theme. What follows is an animal fable reminiscent of La Fontaine's "The Bat and the Two Weasels" (La Fontaine, *Fables*, II-v), recorded in 1947 in a Cameroonian city. The audience was extremely heterogeneous in its linguistic composition. Thus the speaker expressed himself in a mixture cleverly dosed with Army French and pidgin. I must stress that he remained in control of his medium and that the mistakes are only apparent, or rather exist only for a European audience. The speaker deliberately used these "mistakes" for a stylistic effect, a satirical vehicle (he caricatures the French spoken by African police officers, who are recruited in the unschooled north and are almost totally illiterate)—and as a veil for this satire! The traditional theme has been lifted into the colonial social context: the listeners, aware of the traditional theme, delight in this reinterpretation, identifying with the hero. One curious thing, and this may seem to contradict partially what I said above (but, rather, it simply proves that the two literary forms remain complementary), is that the story retains some of its delightful quality even in transcription. But let the reader judge for himself.

La Chauve-Souris et le Recensement

Long, long time fo' old, y a gouverneur pour tous les bêtes y dit tous les Commandants «Vous c'est faire 'censement pour tous les bêtes y courent la forêt, la brousse. Small small beef, big beef, tout ça y court par terre, y grimpe les arbres, c'est payer l'impôt, one time!»

Commandant pour la forêt, c'est Panthère. He call for police, one time, y dit «Tous les bêtes y courent, l'a pas ticket l'impôt, tu dém.... tu prends, tu fous la boîte, y portent l'eau pour Madame Commandant. Go!»

Police c'est Gorille. Y court la forêt, y monte les arbres, y tombe les marigots, y casse son gueule, y fatigue trop. Tous les big beef y zentend lui, y voit lui, c'est dém...sauver, cacher la brousse, pas payer l'impôt. Y continue, continue, continue, jusqu'à fatiguer, y finit trouver Saussouris. Lui c'est pas sauver, pas courir, y reste, y dit Gorille «I see you, Gorille, comment çà va?», plenty pass fine.

Gorille y dit lui «No palaver! toi c'est montrer ticket l'impôt». Saussouris c'est dire «No life ticket l'impôt» Gorille y dit «Quoi c'est! Tous les bêtes y courent la forêt, small beef, big beef c'est faire censement, payer l'impôt». Saussouris y dit «Moi c'est pas la bête y court la forêt, moi c'est l'oiseau».

«C'est pas l'oiseau, y dit Gorille, c'est la bête, c'est payer l'impôt tout suite, j'y fous la boîte!». Saussouris il ouvre les ailes, comme ça, il envole même chose l'oiseau. Gorille il est c... trop.

Quand c'est fini pleuvoir, Gouverneur y dit «Maintenant c'est faire 'censement tous les oiseaux, y a payer l'impôt one time!».

Panthère y call fo' police pour z-oiseau, c'est Obam [Fang : épervier], y dit, «Toi c'est dém.... tous les oiseaux y a ticket l'impôt. Les oiseaux y a pas, tu fous la boîte!».

Obam y vole, y prend tous les petits l'oiseau, y fait 'censement, tous c'est payer l'impôt. Y va, y trouve Saussouris c'est manger les mangues, grand l'arbre, tout l'en haut, l'en haut. Obam y dit «Où ça ticket l'impôt ?».

Saussouris y dit «No life ticket l'impôt!» Obam y dit «Faire 'censement, tous les oiseaux c'est pas payer l'impôt, j'y fous la boîte.» Saussouris y dit «Moi c'est pas l'oiseau, moi c'est la bête.» Y mont'e, y a le poil pour lui, full up, le ventre, le dos... partout. Y mont'e bangala pour lui, même chose le singe, y mont'e zoreilles pour lui, même chose le beef. Obam, y gueule un peu, un peu, y fout le camp.

Saussouris c'est marrer trop.

THE BAT AND THE CENSUS

Once upon a time the great governor of animals told his D.O.'s [district officers], "You make a census of all animals, who dwell in the bush and the forest. Tiny ones, big ones, those who roam around, those who climb the trees, they must pay taxes, at once!"

The D.O. in the forest, that's Panther. He sends for his policeman; he tells him, "All vagrant animals, those who have no tax receipt, you go catch them, you throw them in the calaboose, they bear water for Mrs. D.O. Go!"

The policeman, that's Gorilla. He runs all around the forest. He climbs trees, he falls in rivers. He tries too much. All the big animals, they see him, they hear him, they manage to run away, they hide in the bush, they don't pay taxes. He goes on, and on, and on, till exhaustion. He ends up by meeting Fruit-bat. Fruit-bat does not flee, does not run away. He stays put, tells Gorilla, "I see you, Gorilla. How do you do?" Very nicely.

Gorilla tells him: "No palaver! You show me your tax receipt." Fruit-bat answers: "I have not got one." Gorilla says, "What? All animals in the forest, big ones, small ones, they must get counted. They ought to pay taxes." Fruit-bat says, "I am not a forest-dwelling animal. I am a bird."

"You're no bird," says Gorilla. "You're an animal. You pay taxes at once, or else I throw you in the clink." Fruit-bat opens his wings, so! He flies away like a bird. Gorilla is dumbfounded.

When the rains are over, the Governor say, "Now you make a census of all birds, so that they pay their taxes at once."

Panther sends for the policebird, that's Hawk, and tells him, "You find a way so that all birds have their tax receipt. Those who do not have one you throw in jail!"

Hawk flies around, catches all small birds, makes a census, they all have to pay taxes. He goes and finds Fruit-bat eating mangoes up a big tree. Hawk tells him, "Where's your tax receipt?"

Fruit-bat answers: "I have no tax receipt!" Hawk answers, "I'm census officer. All birds who don't pay taxes, I throw them in the calaboose." Fruit-bat says, "I'm no bird, I'm an animal." He shows how he has got hair everywhere, on his belly, on his back, all over. He shows his genitals, like a monkey's, his ears, like a cow's.

Hawk hollers a bit, then scrams off. Fruit-bat laughs quite a lot.

CHAPTER VI

Since We Must Conclude...
Join Linguistics and See the World!

By the end of this book the European reader should have gained a sketchy acquaintance with African languages, and the African reader with linguistics. I hope I have disgusted neither party, African or European. My purpose in writing this introduction to African languages was first to arouse interest and, if possible, understanding. Both are quite essential in view of all that remains to be done, of all the problems to be resolved in the field of human communication in Africa and with Africa.

It is important to underline the fact that these problems will not be effectively resolved unless they are studied by competent specialists, in the spirit of dispassionate scientific objectivity, purged of all a priori ideology or passion (which does not necessarily exclude understanding). This is not always easy, as it concerns an activity—speech—which reaches into the deepest part of man and which, from the very fact that we all practice it, may appear deceptively simple. Yet, once again, one cannot just drift into linguistics; mastery in this field requires difficult training, particularly for African linguistics, a field which is still searching to define itself, to explore its field of study and its methods. It is precisely this aspect which gives it charm and interest in my eyes.

We should not, however, exaggerate the difficulties involved. If certain aspects, such as that of tone, have barely been clarified at this point, or barely formulated, as in the case of rhythm, the knowledge acquired by general modern linguistics is nonetheless applicable to the study of the languages of Africa and remains a solid and indispensable basis for those who wish to enter this field. Linguistics as a discipline is much less esoteric than it appears at first glance, and its rigorousness, greater than that of other social sciences (while it nevertheless touches all sciences), facilitates the apprenticeship of those who are willing to make the necessary initial effort.

Unfortunately, at the time that I am writing this, few students at the University of Paris have consented to make this effort; since reorganization of the African section of the School of Oriental Languages in 1958, the number of students in African linguistics has never been more than one-tenth that of the students in African anthropology, sociology, geography, and, more recently, history. This is true despite the fact that, precisely because there are so few of them, the positions open to linguists are more numerous than those open to other specialists. This absence of francophonic African linguists poses serious problems at a time when specific programs are just getting under way in theoretical or applied research concerning the languages spoken in the former French colonies. At the same time, in England, America, Germany, and the Soviet Union, as well as in Ghana, Nigeria, and Sierra Leone (to mention only those countries with which I am familiar), teaching and research have greatly developed. In 1964 there were more teachers of African linguistics at the University of London alone than qualified students and researchers in France and francophone Africa combined.

On a completely different level, anyone who wishes seriously to interest himself in African cultural values (which are described by the umbrella terms of "Negritude" or "African personality") must—I repeat, must—divorce himself completely from sentimental exoticism, folklore, or condescension. The scientific study of African languages is not, to be sure, in itself an absolute guarantee of this divorce. The effort it necessitates and the rather radical cultural adjustment which it imposes nevertheless contribute to weeding out the dilettantes and those not seriously interested. One might succeed in passing off a piece of pedantic pseudoscientific journalese as an anthropological study, but it would be much more difficult to do this with a linguistic description.

Finally, let me conclude on a question of politeness and good up-bringing. For more than two centuries (establishment of the Company of Senegal: 1626) Africans have been learning French. Perhaps it is time that more Frenchmen attempt, or reattempt, to learn African languages. Failing this, Africans desiring scientific training in the study of their own languages will do so at London, Leningrad, or Northwestern University.

Selected Bibliography

CHAPTER I

A. MEILLET and M. COHEN, *Les Langues du monde*. 2d ed. Paris, 1948. Chapters: "Langues du Soudan et de la Guinée" (M. DELAFOSSE, redone by A. CAQUOT) and "Langues bantou" and "Langues Khoin" (G. VAN BULCK).

J. GREENBERG, *Languages of Africa*. Bloomington, Ind., 1963.

INTERNATIONAL AFRICAN INSTITUTE, *Handbook of African Languages*. London. See especially the volumes *The Bantu Languages of Africa* (M. A. BRYAN, 1959), *Languages of West Africa* (D. WESTERMANN and M. A. BRYAN, 1952), and *The Non-Bantu Languages of North-Eastern Africa* (A. N. TUCKER and M. A. BRYAN, 1956).

H. BAUMANN, D. WESTERMANN, and P. THURNWALD, *Les peuples et les civilisations de l'Afrique*. Paris, 1948.

CHAPTER II

On the history of African linguistics, see the introduction to the chapter by DELAFOSSE, in *Les langues du monde*, and:

G. VAN BULCK, *Manuel de linguistique bantoue*. Brussels, 1948.

On the techniques and results of modern linguistics:

J. PERROT, *La linguistique*, "Que sais-je?" no. 570. Paris, 1957.

A. MARTINET, *Eléments de linguistique générale*. Paris, 1960. (An especially good source.)

On methods of transcription:

INTERNATIONAL AFRICAN INSTITUTE, *A Practical Orthography for African Languages*. London, 1930. (Translated into French and German.)

Chapter III

Works cited for Chapter I. Also:

I. Ward and D. Westermann, *Practical Phonetics for the Student of African Languages*. London, 1930.

On tones:

K. L. Pike, *Tone Languages*. Ann Arbor, 1948.

On Swahili:

C. Sacleux, *Dictionnaire swahili-français et français-swahili*. 2 vols. Paris, 1941–49.

E. O. Ashton, *Swahili Grammar*. London, 1961. (Very complete but disorganized; serves as the base for the Linguaphone method of Swahili.)

On Bulu:

My own *Manuel élémentaire de langue bulu*. Paris, 1956. (All too elementary.)

On Hausa:

R. C. Abraham, *Dictionary of the Hausa Language*. 2d ed. London, 1962.

There is no really good grammar; if necessary, use:

C. H. Robinson, *Grammar of Hausa*. Cambridge, 1959.
F. W. Taylor, *Practical Hausa Grammar*. London, 1959.

Or, as an introduction,

J. L. Maxwell, and E. M. Forshey, *Yau da gobe*. Lagos, n.d.

On Yoruba:

R. C. Abraham, *Dictionary of Modern Yoruba*. London, 1958.
I. C. Ward, *Introduction to the Yoruba Language*. Cambridge, 1956.

On Fulfulde:

H. Labouret, *La Langue des Peuls ou Foulbe*. Dakar, 1952.
F. W. Taylor, *Fulani-English Dictionary*. London, 1932.
———. *Grammar of the Adamawa Dialect of the Fulani Language*. London, 1953.

On Songhaï:

A. Prost, *La langue songhay et ses dialectes*. Dakar, 1956.

On Mande:

M. Delafosse, *La langue mandingue et ses dialectes*. 2 vols. Paris, 1928–55.

(Notice the small number of French works.)

G. P. Murdock, *Africa, Its Peoples and Their Culture History*. New York, 1959. (Use with great caution.)

M. GUTHRIE, "Bantu Origins: A Tentative New Hypothesis," *Journal of African Languages*, Vol. I. London, 1962. (Difficult but captivating.)

CHAPTER IV

For a rather polemic viewpoint, very representative of nationalist African opinion but with insufficient technical grounding, see CHEIKH ANTA DIOP, *Nations nègres et cultures* (Paris, 1954), in many respects one of the most important books of the past decade. Also the collection of *Présence Africaine*, in particular D. F. SAKILIBA, "Présent et futur des langues africaines," no. 13 (April–May, 1957); my own "Sur la linguistique africaine" (new series, 2d trimester, 1962); and *Actes du deuxième Congrès des Ecrivains et Artistes Noirs*, nos. 24–25 and 27–28 (February–March and August–November, 1959).

Also by me (my apologies, but I am one of the rare scholars in France concerned with this problem): "L'unité linguistique de l'Afrique est-elle possible?" *Tam-Tam*, special number 3–4 (April, 1964) (a very brief synthetic article); "Problèmes linguistiques des états africains à l'heure de l'Indépendance," *Cahiers d'Etudes Africaines*, II-ii, 6 (1961); "Sur les possibilités expressives des langues africaines en matière de terminologie politique," *L'Afrique et l'Asie*, IV: 56 (1961); "L'avenir de la langue française en Afrique noire," *Europe-France-Outremer*, no. 396 (January, 1963).

In English:

J. SPENCER, ed., *Language in Africa* (Cambridge, 1963), and W. H. WHITELEY, "Political Concepts and Connotations . . . in Swahili" (St. Antony's Papers, no. 10), *African Affairs*, I (London, 1961).

CHAPTER V

On the role and importance of words, all the works of MARCEL GRIAULE and his school; the most recent is:

D. ZAHAN, *La dialectique du verbe chez les Bambara*. Paris, 1963.

For a very different (and much more general) approach:

M. COHEN, *Pour une sociologie du langage*. Paris, 1956.

On African literature, the best general introduction is found in the articles by G. BALANDIER in *Histoire Générale des Littératures, Encyclopédie de la Pléiade*; by P. F. LACROIX in *Encyclopédie Quillet*; and—again!—my own *Encyclopédie "Clartés*," Section 15 350.

On the writing systems: see BAUMANN and WESTERMANN, *op. cit.*, Part II. There is a good résumé in TH. MONOD, *L'hippopotame et le philosophe*, 2d ed. (uncensored) (Paris, 1946). *La Grande Chronique du royaume de Foumban*, compiled by order of Sultan Njoya in the writing he had invented, has been translated into French by The Reverend MARTIN (Dakar, 1949).

Talking drums: see the article "*ǹkúl*" in the *Dictionnaire ewondo-français* by the Abbé TH. TSALA (Lyon, n.d. [circa 1950?]). "Le tambour d'appel des Ewôndô," by R. P. L. GUILLEMIN, *Bulletin de la Société d'Etudes Cameroun-aises*, no. 21–22 (1948), is excellent but impossible to find.

Oral poetry: The best collection to appear in French is E. DE DAMPIERRE, *Poètes nzakara* (Paris, 1963), the first volume in the Julliard "Classiques Africains," where the poems are presented in the original languages with the translation on the opposite page; also gives ethnographic and linguistic commentaries. See also O. BÂ, "Dix-huit poèmes peul modernes," presented by P. F. LACROIX, in *Cahiers d'Etudes Africaines*, no. 8, Vol. II-iv (Paris, 1962).

CHAPTER VI

Yearly presentations of the Ecole des Langues Orientales and of the Ecole Pratique des Hautes Etudes.

Addendum (1966): G. CALAME-GRIAULE, *Ethnologie et langage: la parole chez les Dogon* (Paris, 1966). In the collection "Classiques Africains," the volumes on Fulani poetry by P. F. LACROIX, *Poésie peule de l'Adamawa* (Paris, 1965), and by I. SOW, *Chroniques et récits du Foûta Djallon* (Paris, 1968). Finally, S.M. ENO BELINGA, *Littérature et musique populaires en Afrique Noire* (Paris, 1966) (with a recording providing sound illustration: *Chantefables du Cameroun*, "Chant du Monde").

Appendix

SPECIAL CHARACTERS MOST FREQUENTLY USED IN THE TRANSCRIPTION OF AFRICAN LANGUAGES

Most modern transcriptions of African languages, whether they are phonetic or phonological, use special typographic characters based on the rules adopted by the International African Institute, a system inspired by the International Phonetic Alphabet.

The most current signs are:

ə, for mute *e* or schwa
ɔ, for an open *o*, as in "bought" [bɔt]
ɛ, for an open *e*, as in "set" [sɛt]
ʔ, glottal stop
ŋ, velar nasal, pronounced like the *ng*'s in "song" [sɔŋ] or "singer" [siŋər]
ƙ, ɗ, ɓ, "ejective" or glottalized consonants, with no equivalent in Western European languages
~ when used over a vowel indicates nasalization, as in the French "bon" [bɔ̃]. Before a consonant it indicates nasal articulation corresponding to that of the consonant which it precedes: ~*b* = [ᵐb], ~*d* = [ⁿd], etc.

Accent marks indicate tones: ´ high; ` low; ^ falling; ˇ rising. *Over* a vowel, ǀ indicates a mid-tone; *preceding* any character, it marks the tonic accent. š refers to the voiceless sibilant: "ship" (šip), "dish" [diš].

Some ordinary characters have been used, although they have a different value than in English:

c: voiceless affricate, "ch" as in "church" [cərc]
j: voiced affricate: English "Jim" [jim]
u: always "oo": "loop" [lup]
s: always voiceless, as in "see," "pass"

e: French "e with an acute accent": "abbé" [*abe*]
x: velar fricative, voiceless: German "nach" [*nax*]

Small capital letters are sometimes used to differentiate between similar but not identical phonemes: example: R ≠ *r*, to distinguish /*r*/ as uvular from trilled *r*.

For the complete system of transcription see Westermann and Ward, *Practical Phonetics for the Students of African Languages* (London, 1930).

Index

Adult literacy, relationship of, to vernacular languages, 96

African languages: and continental linguistic unity, 83; estimates on numbers of, 1–2; methods of classification of, 62–64; methods of studying, 22–23; missionary effects on, 78n; myths concerning relationship of, to physical type or civilization, 75; and social change resultant on colonial policy, 78. *See also* Classifications of African languages

African linguistics: historical origins of, 19–21; methods of research in, 22–23, 26–27; practical applications of, 23–24; relationship of, to slave trade, 21, 76–77

Afro-Asiatic, 2, 32, 49, 70

Ajami, 20, 108n

Arabic, 2, 4, 17, 32, 53, 97, 108

Armstrong, Robert F., 39

Bambara, 53

Bamoun, 109–10. *See also* Njoya the Great

Bantu languages, 21–22, 35, 37, 39–46, 70, 75

Berber, 2

Bleek, Wilhelm, 21. *See also* Bantu languages

Bloomfield, Leonard, 26

Boas, Franz, 29

Bryan, M. A., 2, 68, 70

Bulu, 34, 36, 44

Bushmen, 33, 75. *See also* Click languages

Class languages, 37, 39–48

Classifications of African languages, 2, 62–64. *See also* Bleek; Bryan; Guthrie; Koelle; Westermann

Click languages, 35

Coast English (Kos Inglisi), 59. *See also* Pidgins

Colonial(ism): attitudes to local-language learning for administration, 80; effect of linguistic decisions of, on African language patterns, 79–80; and foreign-language teaching methods, 84; language policies and differential results in English and French Africa, 80, 98; and international communication, 83; relationship of Belgian, to African languages, 80n; relationship of British and German, to African languages, 79; relationship of French, to African languages, 76–79

"Common Negro African," 82

Crowther, Samuel Ajayi: transcription of Yoruba, 57

Delafosse, Maurice, 1, 3; and Bantu-Sudanic relationship, 22, 65; classification by, 4, 65–66; classification for Hausa, 49; differences of, from Greenberg, 70; Mande dictionary by, 33

Dialectal particularism, 98. *See also* Linguistic nationalism

Doke, Clement, 22

Drummed languages, 113–16. *See also* Music; Tones in African languages; Whistled or shouted languages

Ethnolinguistics, 30, 103

European languages: and comparison between French and English, 98; and contemporary African literature, 118–19; and dialectalization through contact with African languages, 99; and educational development, 78–79, 96; and Pan-Africanism, 81

Ewe, 4

Fulani (Fulfulde), 2, 4, 17, 39, 46–48, 83

Ge'ez (classical Ethiopian), 32
Gouffé, Claude, 39
Greenberg, J. H., 2, 5, 32, 44, 49, 63–64, 68–70, 72n, 75, 76
Guthrie, Malcolm, 2, 43, 45, 65, 70–72, 72n

Hadza, 35. *See also* Click languages
Hausa, 3, 4, 17, 20, 32, 33, 39, 48–53, 83, 84
Hlonipha, 105. *See also* Vernacular language learning rules
Homburger, Lilias, 22, 45, 65
Hottentots, 35, 75. *See also* Click languages
Houis, Maurice, 39

Indigenous scripts, 109. *See also* Bamoun; Nsibidi; Vai

Johnston, Sir Harry, 22

Kaaloŋ, 3
Kikongo, 20, 33
Kinyarwanda, 4, 84n
Kirundi, 4, 84n
Kitchen Kaffir (Isipiki, Fanekalo), 59n. *See also* Pidgins
Koelle, S. W., 21
Krio, 59. *See also* Pidgins
Kriyol, 59. *See also* Pidgins
Kwa group. *See* Yoruba

Lacroix, Pierre F., 39
Language change: in contemporary Africa, 99–102; and population movements, 73–74
Language spread, 3–4
Lexicostatistics, 64
Linguistic nationalism, 82

Magic: relationship of, to language, 106–7. *See also* Secret languages
Mande (Mandinka, Mande-Dyula), 1, 3, 4, 17, 33, 54–56, 60, 83
Meillet, Antoine, 22
Meinhof, Carl, 21, 64–65
Migeod, F. W., 22
Missionaries: creation of "seminary dialects" by, 78n; early linguistic studies by, 20–21; and orthography and standardization, 4
Multilingualism, 16; and problems of national development, 86–87; reasons for, 16–17; relationship of, to population movements, 74
Murdock, G. P., 70
Music: relationship of, to oral literature, 111. *See also* Drummed languages

Nationalism: and African linguistic unification, 83; and choice of national African language, 86–87, 101; and contemporary language-teaching policies, 95; and use of African languages, 81, 82, 84, 84n, 87–88, 101, 102
Nguni, 35. *See also* Click languages
Njoya the Great, 109–10. *See also* Bamoun; Indigenous scripts
Nsibidi, 109–10. *See also* Indigenous scripts
Numbering systems in vernacular languages, 106

Oral literature, 97–111. *See also* Music
Oratorical art, 107. *See also* Oral literature

Pidgins, 5, 17, 59–62, 76
Proto-writing, 110. *See also* Secret languages
Pygmy, 74–75

Sandawe, 35. *See also* Click languages
Sango, 4, 84n
Sapir, Edward, 29
Sara, 5
Secret languages, 106–7
Senghor, Leopold Sedar, 82
Slave trade, 20, 76–77
Sociolinguistics, 81, 82; and contemporary African linguistic stratigraphy, 87; and European languages of communication, 86, 95–96; relationship of, to contemporary African literature, 119; relationship of, to contemporary oral literature, 117
Songhaï-Jerma, 4, 39, 53–54
Sotho-Tswana, 35. *See also* Click languages

Swahili, 3, 4, 17, 20, 25–26, 33, 39, 83–84

Tem, 2
Tones, 35–37, 39; in drummed languages, 113–14
Tucker, A. N., 5, 68, 70
Twi, 2

Vai, 110. *See also* Indigenous scripts
Vernacular language learning rules, 104–6

Vetralla, Father Jacinto Brusciotto di, 20

Ward, Ida, 22
Westermann, D., 1, 2, 5, 21, 22, 49, 66, 76
Whistled or shouted languages, 116. *See also* Drummed languages; Music
Wolof, 60, 83

Yoruba, 3, 17, 56–59, 57, 83, 116